DEEP LEARNING ON EDGE COMPUTING DEVICES

DEEP LEARNING ON EDGE COMPUTING DEVICES

Design Challenges of Algorithm and Architecture

XICHUAN ZHOU

HAIJUN LIU

CONG SHI

JI LIU

Elsevier
Radarweg 29, PO Box 211, 1000 AE Amsterdam, Netherlands
The Boulevard, Langford Lane, Kidlington, Oxford OX5 1GB, United Kingdom
50 Hampshire Street, 5th Floor, Cambridge, MA 02139, United States

Notices

Knowledge and best practice in this field are constantly changing. As new research and experience broaden our understanding, changes in research methods, professional practices, or medical treatment may become necessary.

Practitioners and researchers must always rely on their own experience and knowledge in evaluating and using any information, methods, compounds, or experiments described herein. In using such information or methods they should be mindful of their own safety and the safety of others, including parties for whom they have a professional responsibility.

To the fullest extent of the law, neither the Publisher nor the authors, contributors, or editors, assume any liability for any injury and/or damage to persons or property as a matter of products liability, negligence or otherwise, or from any use or operation of any methods, products, instructions, or ideas contained in the material herein.

Library of Congress Cataloging-in-Publication Data
A catalog record for this book is available from the Library of Congress

British Library Cataloguing-in-Publication Data
A catalogue record for this book is available from the British Library

ISBN: 978-0-323-85783-3

For information on all Elsevier publications
visit our website at https://www.elsevier.com/books-and-journals

Publisher: Mara Conner
Acquisitions Editor: Glyn Jones
Editorial Project Manager: Naomi Robertson
Production Project Manager: Selvaraj Raviraj
Designer: Christian J. Bilbow

Typeset by VTeX

Working together
to grow libraries in
developing countries

www.elsevier.com • www.bookaid.org

Contents

Preface

We first started working in the field of edge computing-based machine learning in 2010. With project funding, we tried to accelerate support vector machine algorithms on integrated circuit chips to support embedded applications such as fingerprint recognition. In recent years, with the development of deep learning and integrated circuit technology, artificial intelligence applications based on edge computing devices, such as intelligent terminals, autonomous driving, and AIOT, are emerging one after another. However, the realization of an embedded artificial intelligence application involves multidisciplinary knowledge of mathematics, computing science, computer architecture, and circuit and system design. Therefore we arrived at the idea of writing a monograph focusing on the research progress of relevant technologies, so as to facilitate the understanding and learning of graduate students and engineers in related fields.

Deep learning application development based on embedded devices is facing the theoretical bottleneck of high complexity of deep neural network algorithms. Realizing the lightweight of various fast developing deep learning models is one of the keys to realize AIOT pervasive artificial intelligence in the future. In recent years, we have been focusing on the development of automated deep learning tools for embedded devices. This book covers some of the cutting-edge technologies, currently developing in embedded deep learning, and introduces some core algorithms, including lightweight neural network design, model compression, model quantization, etc., aiming to provide reference for the readers to design embedded deep learning algorithm.

Deep learning application development based on embedded devices is facing the technical challenge of limited development of integrated circuit technology in the post-Moore era. To address this challenge, in this book, we propose and elaborate a new paradigm of algorithm-hardware codesign to realize the optimization of energy efficiency and performance of neural network computing in embedded devices. The DANoC sparse coding neural network chip developed by us is taken as an example to introduce the new technology of memory computing, hoping to give inspiration to embedded design experts. We believe that, in the post-Moore era, the system collaborative design method across multiple levels of algorithms, software, and hardware will gradually become the mainstream of embedded intelligent design to meet the design requirements of high real-time performance and low power consumption under the condition of limited hardware resources.

Due to time constraints and the authors' limited knowledge, there may be some omissions in the content, and we apologize to the readers for this.

Xichuan Zhou

Acknowledgements

First of all, we would like to thank all the students who participated in the relevant work for their contributions to this book, including Shuai Zhang, Kui Liu, Rui Ding, Shengli Li, Songhong Liang, Yuran Hu, etc.

We would like to take the opportunity to thank our families, friends, and colleagues for their support in the course of writing this monograph. We would also like to thank our organization, School of Microelectronics and Communication Engineering, Chongqing University, for providing supportive conditions to do research on intelligence edge computing.

The main content of this book is compiled from a series of research, partly supported by the National Natural Science Foundation of China (Nos. 61971072 and 62001063).

We are most grateful to the editorial staff and artists at Elsevier and Tsinghua University Press for giving us all the support and assistance needed in the course of writing this book.

PART 1

Introduction

CHAPTER 1

Introduction

1.1 Background

At present, the human society is rapidly entering the era of Internet of Everything. The application of the Internet of Things based on the smart embedded device is exploding. The report "The mobile economy 2020" released by Global System for Mobile Communications Assembly (GSMA) has shown that the total number of connected devices in the global Internet of Things reached 12 billion in 2019 [1]. It is estimated that by 2025 the total scale of the connected devices in the global Internet of Things will reach 24.6 billion. Applications such as smart terminals, smart voice assistants, and smart driving will dramatically improve the organizational efficiency of the human society and change people's lives. With the rapid development of artificial intelligence technology toward pervasive intelligence, the smart terminal devices will further deeply penetrate the human society.

Looking back at the development process of artificial intelligence, at a key time point in 1936, British mathematician Alan Turing proposed an ideal computer model, the general Turing machine, which provided a theoretical basis for the ENIAC (Electronic Numerical Integrator And Computer) born ten years later. During the same period, inspired by the behavior of the human brain, American scientist John von Neumann wrote the monograph "The Computer and the Brain" [2] and proposed an improved stored program computer for ENIAC, i.e., Von Neumann Architecture, which became a prototype for computers and even artificial intelligence systems.

The earliest description of artificial intelligence can be traced back to the Turing test [3] in 1950. Turing pointed out that "if a machine talks with a person through a specific device without communication with the outside, and the person cannot reliably tell that the talk object is a machine or a person, this machine has humanoid intelligence". The word "artificial intelligence" actually appeared at the Dartmouth symposium held by John McCarthy in 1956 [4]. The "father of artificial intelligence" defined it as "the science and engineering of manufacturing smart machines". The proposal of artificial intelligence has opened up a new field. Since then, the

Deep Learning on Edge Computing Devices
https://doi.org/10.1016/B978-0-32-385783-3.00008-9

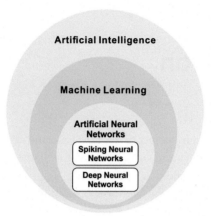

Figure 1.1 Relationship diagram of deep learning related research fields.

academia has also successively presented research results of artificial intelligence. After several historical cycles of development, at present, artificial intelligence has entered a new era of machine learning.

As shown in Fig. 1.1, machine learning is a subfield of theoretical research on artificial intelligence, which has developed rapidly in recent years. Arthur Samuel proposed the concept of machine learning in 1959 and conceived the establishment of a theoretical method "to allow the computer to learn and work autonomously without relying on certain coded instructions" [5]. A representative method in the field of machine learning is the support vector machine [6] proposed by Russian statistician Vladimir Vapnik in 1995. As a data-driven method, the statistics-based SVM has perfect theoretical support and excellent model generalization ability, and is widely used in scenarios such as face recognition.

Artificial neural network (ANN) is one of the methods to realize machine learning. The artificial neural network uses the structural and functional features of the biological neural network to build mathematical models for estimating or approximating functions. ANNs are computing systems inspired by the biological neural networks that constitute animal brains. An ANN is based on a collection of connected units or nodes called artificial neurons, which loosely model the neurons in a biological brain. The concept of the artificial neural network can be traced back to the neuron model (MP model) [7] proposed by Warren McCulloch and Walter Pitts in 1943. In this model the input multidimensional data are multiplied by the corresponding weight parameters and accumulated, and the accumulated value is calculated by a specific threshold function to output the prediction result. Later, Frank Rosenblatt built a perceptron system [8] with two layers of neurons in 1958, but the perceptron model and its subsequent improvement methods had limitations in solving high-dimensional nonlinear problems. Until 1986, Geoffrey Hinton, a professor in the Department of Computer Science at the University of Toronto, invented the back propagation algorithm [9] for parameter estimation of the artificial neural network and realized the training of the multilayer neural networks.

As a branch of the neural network technology, the deep learning technology has been a great success in recent years. The algorithmic milestone appeared in 2006. Hinton invented the Boltzmann machine and successfully solved the problem [10] of vanishing gradients in training the multilayer neural networks. So far, the artificial neural network has officially entered the "deep" era. In 2012, the convolutional neural network [11] and its variants invented by Professor Yann LeCun from New York University greatly improved the classification accuracy of the machine learning methods on large-scale image databases and reached and surpassed people's image recognition level in the following years, which laid the technical foundation for the large-scale industrial application of the deep learning technology. At present, the deep learning technology is ever developing rapidly and achieved great success in subdivision fields of machine vision [12] and voice processing [13]. Especially in 2016, Demis Hassabis's Alpha Go artificial intelligence built based on the deep learning technology defeated Shishi Li, the international Go champion by 4:1, which marked that artificial intelligence has entered a new era of rapid development.

1.2 Applications and trends

The Internet of Things technology is considered to be one of the important forces that lead to the next wave of industrial change. The concept of the Internet of Things was first proposed by Kevin Ashton of MIT in 2009. He pointed out that "the computer can observe and understand the world by RF transmission and sensor technology, i.e., empower computers with their own means of gathering information" [14]. After the massive data collected by various sensors are connected to the network, the connection between human beings and everything is enhanced, thereby expanding the boundaries of the Internet and greatly increasing industrial production efficiency. In the new "wave of industrial technological change", the smart terminal devices will undoubtedly play an important role. As a carrier for connection of Internet of Things, the smart perception terminal device not only realizes data collection, but also has front-end and local data processing capabilities, which can realize the protection of data privacy and the extraction and analysis of perceived semantic information.

With the proposal of the smart terminal technology, the fields of Artificial Intelligence (AI) and Internet of Things (IoT) have gradually merged into the artificial intelligence Internet of Things (AI&IoT or AIoT). On one hand, the application scale of artificial intelligence has been gradually expanded and penetrated into more fields relying on the Internet of Things; on the other hand, the devices of Internet of Things require the embedded smart algorithms to extract valuable information in the front-end collection of sensor data. The concept of intelligence Internet of Things (AIoT) was proposed by the industrial community around 2018 [15], which aimed at realizing the digitization and intelligence of all things based on the edge computing of the Internet of Things terminal. AIoT-oriented smart terminal applications have a period of rapid development. According to a third-party report from iResearch, the total amount of AIoT financing in the Chinese market from 2015 to 2019 was approximately $29 billion, with an increase of 73%.

The first characteristic of AIoT smart terminal applications is the high data volume because the edge has a large number of devices and large size of data. Gartner's report has shown that there are approximately 340,000 autonomous vehicles in the world in 2019, and it is expected that in 2023, there will be more than 740,000 autonomous vehicles with data collection capabilities running in various application scenarios. Taking Tesla as an example, with eight external cameras and one powerful system on chip (SOC) [16], the autonomous vehicles can support end-to-end machine vision image processing to perceive road conditions, surrounding vehicles and the environment. It is reported that a front camera with a resolution of 1280×960 in Tesla Model 3 can generate about 473 GB of image data in one minute. According to the statistics, at present, Tesla has collected more than 1 million video data and labeled the information about distance, acceleration, and speed of 6 billion objects in the video. The data amount is as high as 1.5 PB, which provides a good data basis for improvement of the performance of the autonomous driving artificial intelligence model.

The second characteristic of AIoT smart terminal applications is high latency sensitivity. For example, the vehicle-mounted ADAS of autonomous vehicles has strict requirements on response time from image acquisition and processing to decision making. For example, the average response time of Tesla autopilot emergency brake system is 0.3 s (300 ms), and a skilled driver also needs approximately 0.5 s to 1.5 s. With the data-driven machine learning algorithms, the vehicle-mounted system HW3 proposed by Tesla in 2019 processes 2300 frames per second (fps), which is 21 times higher than the 110 fps image processing capacity of HW2.5.

The third characteristic of AIoT smart terminal applications is high energy efficiency. Because wearable smart devices and smart speakers in embedded artificial intelligence application fields [17] are mainly battery-driven, the power consumption and endurance are particularly critical. Most of the smart speakers use a voice awakening mechanism, which can realize conversion from the standby state to the working state according to the recognition of human voice keywords. Based on the embedded voice recognition artificial intelligence chip with high power efficiency, a novel smart speaker can achieve wake-on-voice at standby power consumption of 0.05 W. In typical offline human–machine voice interaction application scenarios, the power consumption of the chip can also be controlled within 0.7 W, which provides conditions for battery-driven systems to work for a long time. For example, Amazon smart speakers can achieve 8 hours of battery endurance in the always listening mode, and the optimized smart speakers can achieve up to 3 months of endurance.

From the perspective of future development trends, the development goal of the artificial intelligence Internet of Things is achieving ubiquitous pervasive intelligence [18]. The pervasive intelligence technology aims to solve the core technical challenges of high volume, high time sensitivity, and high power efficiency of the embedded smart devices and finally to realize the digitization and intelligence of all things [19]. The basis of development is to understand the legal and ethical relationship between the efficiency improvement brought by the development of the artificial intelligence technology and the protection of personal privacy, so as to improve the efficiency of social production and the convenience of people's lives under the premise of guaranteeing the personal privacy. We believe that pervasive intelligence calculation for the artificial intelligence Internet of Things will become a key technology to promote a new wave of industrial technological revolution.

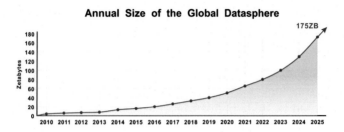

Figure 1.2 Global data growth forecast.

1.3 Concepts and taxonomy

1.3.1 Preliminary concepts

Data, computing power, and algorithms are regarded as three elements that promote the development of artificial intelligence, and the development of these three elements has become a booster for the explosion of the deep learning technology. First of all, the ability to acquire data, especially large-scale data with labels, is a prerequisite for the development of the deep learning technology. According to the statistics, the size of the global Internet data in 2020 has exceeded 30 ZB [20]. Without data optimization and compression, the estimated storage cost alone will exceed RMB 6 trillion, which is equivalent to the sum of GDP of Norway and Austria in 2020. With the further development of the Internet of Things and 5G technology, more data sources and capacity enhancements at the transmission level will be brought. It is foreseeable that the total amount of data will continue to develop rapidly at higher speed. It is estimated that the total amount of data will be 175 ZB by 2025, as shown in Fig. 1.2. The increase in data size provides a good foundation for the performance improvement of deep learning models. On the other hand, the rapidly growing data size also puts forward higher computing performance requirements for model training.

Secondly, the second element of the development of artificial intelligence is the computing system. The computing system refers to the hardware computing devices required to achieve an artificial intelligence system. The computing system is sometimes described as the "engine" that supports the application of artificial intelligence. In the deep learning era of artificial intelligence, the computing system has become an infrastructure resource. When Google's artificial intelligence Alpha Go [21] defeated Korean chess player Shishi Li in 2016, people lamented the powerful artificial intelligence, and the huge "payment" behind it was little known: 1202

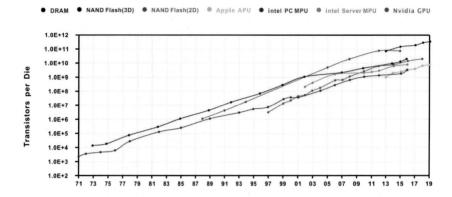

Figure 1.3 Development trend of transistor quantity.

CPUs, 176 high-performance GPUs, and the astonishing power of 233 kW consumed in a game of chess.

From the perspective of the development of the computing system, the development of VLSI chips is the fundamental power for the improvement of AI computing performance. The good news is that although the development of the semiconductor industry has periodic fluctuation, the well-known "Moore's law" [22] in the semiconductor industry has experienced the test for 50 years (Fig. 1.3). Moore's law is still maintained in the field of VLSI chips, largely because the rapid development of GPU has made up for the slow development of CPU. We can see from the figure that in 2010 the number of GPU transistors has grown more than that of CPUs, CPU transistors have begun to lag behind Moore's law, and the development of hardware technologies [23] such as special ASICs for deep learning and FPGA heterogeneous AI computing accelerators have injected new fuel for the increase in artificial intelligence computing power.

Last but not least, the third element of artificial intelligence development is an algorithm. An algorithm is a finite sequence of well-defined, computer-implementable instructions, typically to solve a class of specific problems in finite time. Performance breakthrough in the algorithm and application based on deep learning in the past 10 years is an important reason for the milestone development of AI technology. So, what is the future development trend of deep learning algorithms in the era of Internet of Everything? This problem is one of the core problems discussed in academia and industry. A general consensus is that the deep learning algorithms will develop toward high efficiency.

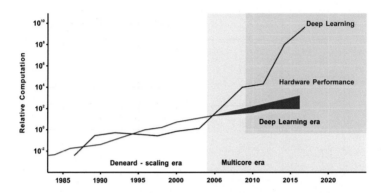

Figure 1.4 Comparison of computing power demands and algorithms for deep learning model.

OpenAI, an open artificial intelligence research organization, has pointed out that "the computing resource required by advanced artificial intelligence doubles approximately every three and a half months". The computing resource of training a large AI model has increased by 300,000 times since 2012, with an average annual increase of 11.5 times. The growth rate of hardware computing performance has only reached an average annual increase of 1.4 times. On the other hand, the improvement of the efficiency of high-efficiency deep learning algorithms reaches annual average saving of about 1.7 times of the computing resource. This means that as we continue to pursue the continuous improvement of algorithm performance, the increase of computing resource demands potentially exceeds the development speed of hardware computing performance, as shown in Fig. 1.4. A practical example is the deep learning model GPT-3 [24] for natural language processing issued in 2020. Only the cost of model training and computing resource deployment has reached about 13 million dollars. If the computing resource cost increases exponentially, then it is difficult to achieve sustainable development. How to solve this problem is one of the key problems in the development of artificial intelligence toward the pervasive intelligence.

1.3.2 Two stages of deep learning: training and inference

Deep learning is generally classified into two stages, training and inference. First, the process of estimating the parameters of the neural network model based on known data is called training. Training is sometimes also known as the process of parameter learning. In this book, to avoid ambiguity, we use the word "training" to describe the parameter estimation process. The data required in the training process is called a training dataset. The training algorithm is usually described as an optimization task. The model parameters with the smallest prediction error of the data labels on the training sample set are estimated through gradient descent [25], and the neural network model with better generalization is acquired through regularization [26].

In the second stage, the trained neural network model is deployed in the system to predict the labels of the unknown data obtained by the sensor in real time. This process is called the inference process. Training and inference of models are like two sides of the same coin, which belong to different stages and are closely related. The training quality of the model determines the inference accuracy of the model.

For the convenience of understanding the subsequent content of this book, we summarize the main concepts of machine learning involved in the training and inference process as follows.

Dataset. The dataset is a collection of known data with similar attributes or features and their labels. In deep learning, signals such as voices and images acquired by the sensor are usually converted into data expression forms of vectors, matrices, or tensors. The dataset is usually classified into a training dataset and a test dataset, which are used for the estimation of the parameters of the neural network model and the evaluation of neural network inference performance respectively.

Deep learning model. In this book, we will name a function $f(\mathbf{x}; \boldsymbol{\theta})$ from the known data $\mathbf{x}$ to the label $\mathbf{y}$ to be estimated as the model, where $\boldsymbol{\theta}$ is a collection of internal parameters of the neural network. It is worth mentioning that in deep learning, the parameters and function forms of the model are diverse and large in scale. It is usually difficult to write the analytical form of the function. Only a formal definition is provided here.

Objective function. The process of deep learning model training is defined as an optimization problem. The objective function of the optimization problem generally includes two parts, a loss function and a regularization term. The loss function is used to describe the average error of the label prediction of the neural network model on the training samples. The loss function is minimized to enhance the accuracy of the model on the training sample set. The regularization term is usually used to control the complexity of the model to improve the accuracy of the model for unknown data labels and the generalization performance of the model.

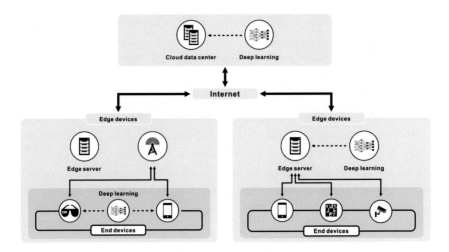

Figure 1.5 Application scenarios of cloud and edge.

1.3.3 Cloud and edge devices

Edge computing [27] refers to a concept in which a distributed architecture decomposes and cuts the large-scale computing of the central node into smaller and easier-to-manage parts and disperses them to the edge nodes for processing. The edge nodes are closer to the terminal devices and have higher transmission speed and lower time delay. As shown in Fig. 1.5, the cloud refers to the central servers far away from users. The users can access these servers anytime and anywhere through the Internet to realize information query and sharing. The edge refers to the base station or server close to the user side. We can see from the figure that the terminal devices [28] such as monitoring cameras, mobile phones, and smart watches are closer to the edge. For deep learning applications, if the inference stage can be completed at the edge, then the problem of transmission time delay may be solved, and the edge computing provides services near data sources or users, which will not cause the problem of privacy disclosure. Data show that cloud computing power will grow linearly in future years, with a compound annual growth rate of 4.6%, whereas demand at the edge is exponential, with a compound annual growth rate of 32.5%.

The edge computing terminal refers to the smart devices that focus on real-time, secure, and efficient specific scenario data analysis on user terminals. The edge computing terminal has huge development prospects in the field of artificial intelligence Internet of Things (AIoT). A large number of sensor devices in the Internet of Things industry need to collect various types of data at high frequency. Edge computing devices can integrate data collection, calculation, and execution to effectively avoid the cost and time delay of uploading the data to cloud computing and improve the security and privacy protection of user data. According to an IDC survey, 45% of the data generated by the Internet of Things industry in 2020 will be processed at the edge of the network, and this proportion will expand in the future years. "2021 Edge Computing Technology White Paper" has pointed out that the typical application scenarios of edge computing smart terminals include smart car networking/autonomous driving, industrial Internet, and smart logistics. The values of ultralow time delay, massive data, edge intelligence, data security, and cloud collaboration will prompt more enterprises to choose edge computing.

1.4 Challenges and objectives

In recent years, deep learning has made breakthroughs in the fields of machine vision and voice recognition. However, because the training and inference of standard deep neural networks involve a large number of parameters and floating-point computing, they usually need to be run on resource-intensive cloud servers and devices. However, this solution has the following two challenges.

(1) Privacy problem. Sending user data (such as photos and voice) to the cloud will cause a serious privacy disclosure problem. The European Union, the United States, etc. have set up strict legal management and monitoring systems for sending the user data to the cloud.

(2) High delay. Many smart terminal applications have extremely high requirements for the end-to-end delay from data collection to completion of processing. However, the end-cloud collaborative architecture has the problem that data transmission delay is uncertain and is difficult to meet the needs of high time sensitivity smart applications such as autonomous driving.

Edge computing effectively solves the above problem and has gradually become a research hotspot. Recently, edge computing has made some breakthroughs in technology. On one hand, algorithm design companies have begun to seek more efficient and lightweight deep learning models (such as MobileNet and ShuffleNet). On the other hand, hardware technology companies, especially chip technology companies, have invested heavily in the development of special neural network computing acceleration chips (such as NPU). How to minimize resource consumption by optimizing algorithms and hardware architecture on edge devices with limited resources is of great significance to the development and the application of AIoT in the 5G and even 6G era.

The deep learning edge computing technology based on smart terminals will effectively solve the above technical challenges of deep learning cloud computing. This book focuses on the deep learning edge computing technology and introduces how to design, optimize, and deploy efficient neural network models on embedded smart terminals from the three levels of algorithms, hardware, and applications. In the algorithm technology, neural network algorithms for edge deep learning is introduced, including lightweight neural network structure design, pruning, and compression technology. The hardware technology details the hardware design and optimization methods of edge deep learning, including algorithm and hardware collaborative design, near memory computing, and hardware implementation of integrated learning. For the application program, each part briefly introduces the application program. In addition, as a comprehensive example, the application of smart monitoring cameras will be introduced as a separate part at the end of this book, which integrates algorithm innovation and hardware architecture innovation.

1.5 Outline of the book

This book aims to comprehensively cover the latest progress in edge-based neural computing, including algorithm models and hardware design. To reflect the needs of the market, in this book, we attempt to systematically summarize the related technologies of edge deep learning, including algorithm models, hardware architectures, and applications. The performance of deep learning models can be maximized on the edge computing devices through collaborative algorithm-hardware-code design.

The structure of this book is as follows. According to the content, it includes three parts and nine chapters. Part 1 is Introduction, including two chapters (Chapters 1–2); Part 2 is Model and Algorithm, including three chapters (Chapters 3–5); and Part 3 is Architecture Optimization, including four chapters (Chapters 6–9).

The first chapter (Introduction) mainly describes the development process, related applications, and development prospects of artificial intelligence, provides some basic concepts and terms in the field of deep learning, and finally provides the research content and contributions of this book.

The second chapter (The Basic of Deep Learning) explains the relevant basis of deep learning, including architectures of feedforward neural networks, convolutional neural networks, and recurrent neural networks, as well as the training process of the network models and performance and challenges of the deep neural networks on AIoT devices.

Chapter 3 (Model Design and Compression) discusses the current lightweight model design and compression methods, including efficient lightweight network designs by presenting some classical lightweight models and the model compression methods by detailedly introducing two typical methods, model pruning and knowledge distillation.

Chapter 4 (Mix-Precision Model Encoding and Quantization) proposes a mixed precision quantization and encoding bitwise bottleneck method from the perspective of quantization and encoding of neural network activation based on the signal compression theory in wireless communication, and can quantify the neural network activation from a floating point type to a low-precision fixed point type. Experiments on ImageNet and other datasets show that by minimizing the quantization distortion of each layer the bitwise bottleneck encoding method realizes state-of-the-art performance with low-precision activation.

Chapter 5 (Model Encoding of Binary Neural Networks) focuses on the binary neural network model and proposes a hardware-friendly method to improve the performance of efficient deep neural networks with binary weights and activation. The cellular binary neural network includes multiple parallel binary neural networks, which optimize the lateral connections through group sparse regularization and knowledge distillation. Experiments on CIFAR-10 and ImageNet datasets show that by introducing optimized group sparse lateral paths the cellular binary neural network can obtain better performance than other binary deep neural networks.

Chapter 6 (Binary Neural Networks Computing Architecture) proposes a fully pipelined BNN accelerator from the perspective of hardware acceleration design, which has a bagging integrated unit for aggregating multiple BNN pipelines to achieve better model precision. Compared with other methods, this design greatly improves memory footprint and power efficiency on the MNIST dataset.

Chapter 7 (Algorithm and Hardware Codesign of Sparse Binary Network-on-Chip) proposes a hardware-oriented deep learning algorithm-deep adaptive network method from the perspective of algorithm and hardware collaborative design to explore the sparsity between neural network connections. To make full use of the advantages of algorithm optimization, we propose an efficient hardware architecture based on a sparsely mapped memory. Unlike the traditional network architecture on chip, the deep adaptive network on chip (DANoC) closely combines communication and calculation to avoid massive power loss caused by parameter transmission between the onboard memory and the on-chip computing unit. The experimental results show that compared with the most advanced method, the system has higher precision and efficiency.

Chapter 8 (Hardware Architecture Optimization for Object Tracking) proposes a low-cost and high-speed VLSI system for object tracking from the perspective of algorithm and hardware collaborative design based on texture and dynamic compression perception features and ellipse matching algorithm. The system introduces a memory-centric architecture mode, multistage pipelines, and parallel processing circuits to achieve high frame rates while consuming minimal hardware resources. Based on the FPGA prototype system, at a clock frequency of 100 MHz, a processing speed of 600 frames per second is realized, and stable tracking results are maintained.

Chapter 9 (SensCamera: A Learning based Smart Camera Prototype) provides an example of edge computing terminals, a smart monitoring camera prototype system from the perspective of algorithm and hardware collaborative design, and integrates algorithm innovation and hardware architecture innovation. First, we propose a hardware-friendly algorithm, which is an efficient convolutional neural network for unifying object detection and image compression. The algorithm uses convolution computation to perform near-isometric compressed perception and invents a new noncoherent convolution method to learn the sampling matrix to realize the near-isometric characteristics of compressed perception. Finally, through hardware-oriented algorithm optimization, a smart camera prototype built with independent hardware can be used to perform object detection and image compression of 20 to 25 frames of video images per second with power consumption of 14 watts.

References

[1] Intelligence-GSMA, The mobile economy 2020, Tech. rep., GSM Association, London, 2020.
[2] J. Von Neumann, The Computer and the Brain, Yale University Press, 2012.

[3] B.G. Buchanan, A (very) brief history of artificial intelligence, AI Magazine 26 (2005) 53–60.

[4] J. McCarthy, M. Minsky, N. Rochester, C.E. Shannon, A proposal for the Dartmouth summer research project on artificial intelligence, August 31, 1955, AI Magazine 27 (2006) 12–14.

[5] A.L. Samuel, Some studies in machine learning using the game of checkers, IBM Journal of Research and Development 3 (1959) 210–229.

[6] C. Cortes, V. Vapnik, Support-vector networks, Machine Learning 20 (3) (1995) 273–297.

[7] W.S. McCulloch, W. Pitts, A logical calculus of the ideas immanent in nervous activity, The Bulletin of Mathematical Biophysics 5 (4) (1943) 115–133.

[8] F. Rosenblatt, The perceptron: a probabilistic model for information storage and organization in the brain, Psychological Review 65 (6) (1958) 386.

[9] D.E. Rumelhart, G.E. Hinton, R.J. Williams, Learning representations by back-propagating errors, Nature 323 (6088) (1986) 533–536.

[10] G.E. Hinton, S. Osindero, Y.-W. Teh, A fast learning algorithm for deep belief nets, Neural Computation 18 (7) (2006) 1527–1554.

[11] Y. LeCun, L. Bottou, Y. Bengio, P. Haffner, Gradient-based learning applied to document recognition, Proceedings of the IEEE 86 (11) (1998) 2278–2324.

[12] A. Voulodimos, N. Doulamis, A. Doulamis, E. Protopapadakis, Deep learning for computer vision: A brief review, Computational Intelligence and Neuroscience (2018).

[13] H. Purwins, B. Li, T. Virtanen, J. Schlüter, S.-y. Chang, T. Sainath, Deep learning for audio signal processing, IEEE Journal of Selected Topics in Signal Processing 13 (2019) 206–219.

[14] K. Ashton, et al., That 'internet of things' thing, RFID Journal 22 (7) (2009) 97–114.

[15] A. Ghosh, D. Chakraborty, A. Law, Artificial intelligence in internet of things, CAAI Transactions on Intelligence Technology 3 (4) (2018) 208–218.

[16] S. Ingle, M. Phute, Tesla autopilot: semi autonomous driving, an uptick for future autonomy, International Research Journal of Engineering and Technology 3 (9) (2016) 369–372.

[17] B. Sudharsan, S.P. Kumar, R. Dhakshinamurthy, AI vision: Smart speaker design and implementation with object detection custom skill and advanced voice interaction capability, in: Proceedings of International Conference on Advanced Computing, 2019, pp. 97–102.

[18] D. Saha, A. Mukherjee, Pervasive computing: a paradigm for the 21st century, Computer 36 (3) (2003) 25–31.

[19] M. Satyanarayanan, Pervasive computing: Vision and challenges, IEEE Personal Communications 8 (4) (2001) 10–17.

[20] D. Reinsel, J. Gantz, J. Rydning, Data age 2025: the evolution of data to life-critical don't focus on big data; focus on the data that's big, Tech. rep., IDC, Seagate, 2017.

[21] S.D. Holcomb, W.K. Porter, S.V. Ault, G. Mao, J. Wang, Overview on DeepMind and its AlphaGo Zero AI, in: Proceedings of the International Conference on Big Data and Education, 2018, pp. 67–71.

[22] R. Schaller, Moore's law: past, present and future, IEEE Spectrum 34 (1997) 52–59.

[23] D. Han, S. Zhou, T. Zhi, Y. Chen, T. Chen, A survey of artificial intelligence chip, Journal of Computer Research and Development 56 (1) (2019) 7.

[24] T.B. Brown, B. Mann, N. Ryder, M. Subbiah, J. Kaplan, et al., Language models are few-shot learners, arXiv:2005.14165 [abs].

[25] J. Zhang, Gradient descent based optimization algorithms for deep learning models training, arXiv:1903.03614 [abs].

[26] J. Kukacka, V. Golkov, D. Cremers, Regularization for deep learning: A taxonomy, arXiv:1710.10686 [abs].

[27] W. Shi, J. Cao, Q. Zhang, Y. Li, L. Xu, Edge computing: Vision and challenges, IEEE Internet of Things Journal 3 (5) (2016) 637–646.

[28] J. Chen, X. Ran, Deep learning with edge computing: A review, Proceedings of the IEEE 107 (8) (2019) 1655–1674.

CHAPTER 2

The basics of deep learning

2.1 Feedforward neural networks

A feedforward neural network (or fully connected neural network) is one of the earliest neural network models invented in the field of artificial intelligence [1]. It is able to learn autonomously via the input data to complete specific tasks. Here we take image classification [2], one of the core problems in the field of computer vision, as an example to illustrate the principle of a feedforward neural network. The so-called classification problem is allocating a label to each input data on the premise of a fixed set of classification labels. The task of a feedforward neural network is predicting the classification label of a given image. The prediction is made by giving scores (prediction probabilities) of the image under each classification label in the form of a vector, which are also the output of the feedforward neural network. Apparently, the label with the highest score is the category to which the network predicts that the image belongs. As shown in Fig. 2.1(b), the process of prediction is a simple linear mapping combined with an activation function σ,

$$f(\mathbf{x}; \mathbf{W}, \mathbf{b}) = \sigma(\mathbf{Wx} + \mathbf{b}), \qquad (2.1)$$

where the image data $\mathbf{x} \in \mathbb{R}^d$, d is the number of pixel elements of the images. The parameters of this linear function are the matrix $\mathbf{W} \in \mathbb{R}^{c \times d}$ and column vector $\mathbf{b} \in \mathbb{R}^c$, and c represents the number of categories. The parameter $\mathbf{W}$ is called the weight, and $\mathbf{b}$ is called the bias vector. Obviously, the weight and bias affect the performance of the feedforward neural network, and the correct prediction is closely related to the values of these two matrix vectors. According to the operational rule of matrices, the output will be a column vector of size $c \times 1$, i.e., the scores of the c categories mentioned earlier.

The structure of the feedforward neural network is inspired by the neuronal system of human brain [3]. The basic unit of computation of the brain is neuron. There are 80 billion neurons in a human neuronal system, which are connected by approximately 10^{14} to 10^{15} synapses. Fig. 2.1(a) shows a biological neuron. As shown in the figure, each neuron receives input signals from its dendrites and then generates output signals along its

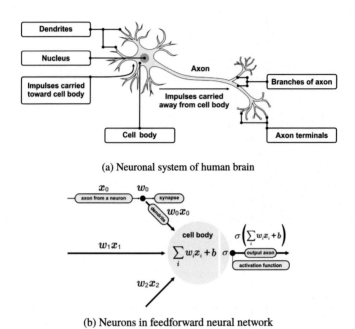

(a) Neuronal system of human brain

(b) Neurons in feedforward neural network

Figure 2.1 The correspondings between the neuronal structure of human brain and the artificial neural network.

unique axon. The axon branches off gradually at the end and is connected to dendrites of other neurons through synapses. In the computation model of an artificial neuron, signals propagating along the axon (equivalent to input **x**) interact with the dendrites of other neurons (equivalent to matrix operation **Wx**) based on the synaptic strength of synapses (equivalent to weight **W**). The synaptic strength can control the strength of influence of one neuron on the other one, as well as the direction of influence: to excite (positive weight) or suppress (negative weight) that neuron. Dendrites transmit signals to a cell body, where the signals are added up.

According to what has been said so far, the human brain system works in a way similar to the linear mapping we just mentioned, but then the crucial point comes. The neurons activate and output an electrical pulse to their axons only if the sum in the cell body is above a certain threshold. In neuronal dynamics, the Leaky Integrate-and-Fire (LIF) model [4] is commonly used to describe this process. The model describes the membrane potential of the neuron based on the input to synapse and the injection current it receives. Simply speaking, the communication between two neurons requires a spike as a mark. When the synapse of the previous neuron sends

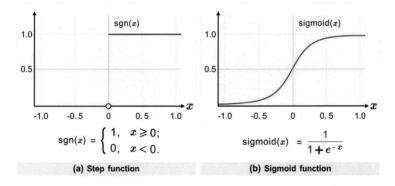

Figure 2.2 The illustration of two activation functions, step and sigmoid functions.

out a current, the membrane potential rises. Once the membrane potential exceeds a given threshold, a spike will be generated, and the membrane potential will be reset. Obviously, this process of spike generation is similar to a threshold-based function. If the current is lower than the threshold, then there will be no spike, and if the current is higher than the threshold, then there will be a spike, which is similar to the characteristics of a step function.

The concept of activation function [5] was proposed in the light of this characteristic of human brain neurons. The activation function makes the neural network nonlinear, so that some problems that linear regression cannot handle can be solved. The step function just mentioned can handle the binary classification problem (outputting "yes" or "no"). For more categories, we need an intermediate activation value or an accurate description of the degree of activation, rather than a simple division into 100% or 0. In such a context, traditional activation functions such as sigmoid were proposed, which normalizes the input to (0, 1), achieves nonlinearity, and has an intermediate activation value. The formulations and curves are shown in Fig. 2.2.

Normally, a typical feedforward neural network has one or more additional layers of neurons between the input and output layers, which are called hidden layers. The hidden layers exist to identify and divide the features of the input data in greater detail [6], so as to make correct predictions. We divide a classification problem into multiple subproblems based on physical features, and each neuron in the hidden layers is responsible for dealing with such a subproblem. Fig. 2.3 shows a three-layer feedforward neural network. The first layer is an input layer, containing three neurons;

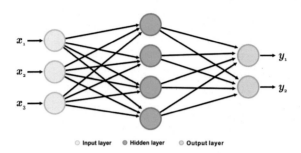

Figure 2.3 Schematic diagram of three-layer feedforward neural network.

the second layer is a hidden layer, containing four neurons; and the third layer is an output layer, containing two neurons. Neurons in two adjacent layers are connected to each other, and neurons in the same layer are not connected. The input layer and hidden layer of the network are used as an example to describe the formula of fully connection:

$$\hat{y}_j = \text{sigmoid}\left(\sum_{i=1}^{3} w_{ij} x_i + b_j\right), \tag{2.2}$$

where w_{ij} represents the weight value between the ith neuron in the input layer and the jth neuron in the hidden layer, and x_i represents the numerical value of the ith element in the input column vector. These two values are multiplied and added to the bias b_j of each neuron in the hidden layer, and the resulting value is processed by the activation function sigmoid. Therefore the output $\hat{y}_j$ of each neuron in the hidden layer can be obtained.

In practical applications, the number of hidden layers can be increased, and the way that the hidden layers are connected will also change, which is the deep neural network to be mentioned later.

2.2 Deep neural networks

2.2.1 Convolutional neural networks

As we mentioned in the previous section, the input to the feedforward neural network is vector data, which will be subjected to feature extraction in multiple hidden layers. Each hidden layer is made up of several neurons, and each neuron is connected to all neurons in the previous layer. The final fully connected layer is called the output layer, and its output values are considered to be the score values for different categories in classification

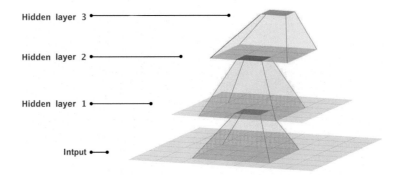

Hidden layer 3

Hidden layer 2

Hidden layer 1

Intput

Figure 2.4 Schematic diagram of convolutional operation receptive field.

problems. Such a kind of network structure has obvious defects when facing large-size image input. The fully connected structure between hidden layers leads to a sharp increase in network parameter numbers, which not only greatly reduces the training speed, but also may lead to overfitting of the network and greatly damage the model performance. The fitting accuracy can be improved by increasing the number of network layers, but with the increase in the number of layers, problems such as gradient vanishing are easy to appear, making it difficult for the network to train convergence.

Patterns of image recognition by human brain have been found to be instructive for the improvement of the structure of artificial neural networks. The human brain first perceives each local feature in the picture and then performs a higher level of integration to obtain global information. This is to make use of the sparse connectivity of the observed objects in the image, that is, local pixels in the image are closely related, whereas the correlation between pixels that are further apart is weak. Like the human brain, we only need to perceive local features of an image at the hidden layers and then integrate the local information at a higher layer to recognize a complete image.

In recent years, it has been found that the convolution operator, which is widely used in the field of signal processing, can complete such a process. For one-dimensional time series signals, convolution is a special integral operation. When extended to a two-dimensional image, a matrix called convolutional kernel will be used to replace a signal participating in convolution in the one-dimensional case [7]. We have each convolutional kernel in the hidden layer connected to only one local area of the input data, and the spatial size of the connection is called the receptive field of the neuron.

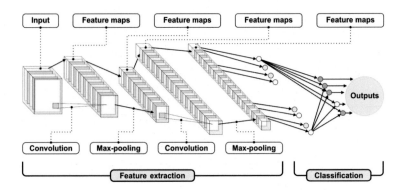

Figure 2.5 The illustration of a typical convolutional neural network structure.

The receptive field can be understood as the size of the area seen by a neuron [8]. The deeper the neuron, the larger the input area that the neuron can see. As shown in Fig. 2.4, the receptive field of each neuron in the first hidden layer is 3, the receptive field of each neuron in the second hidden layer is 5, and the receptive field of each neuron in the third hidden layer is 7. The further away the hidden layer is from the input layer, the more features can be obtained, realizing the control from local features to the whole perception.

The convolutional kernel is equivalent to a mapping rule in which the value of an original image pixel point is multiplied by the value of the convolutional kernel at the corresponding location, and then the resulting values are added according to the weights. This process is similar to the search for a class of patterns in an image to extract the features of the image. Obviously, such a filter is not able to extract all features, and a set of different filters is required.

Convolutional neural network is a kind of feedforward neural networks with convolution operation and deep structure [9]. Its structure, as shown in Fig. 2.5, includes multiple convolutional layers for feature extraction, pooling layers for reducing the amount of computation, and a fully connected neural network layer for classification. We will elaborate on the principles of each layer below.

A convolutional layer is a hidden layer that contains several convolution units in a convolutional neural network, which is used for feature extraction. As mentioned above, the convolution is characterized by sparse connection and parameter sharing. The structure of the convolutional layer is shown in Fig. 2.6. The square window on the left is the previously men-

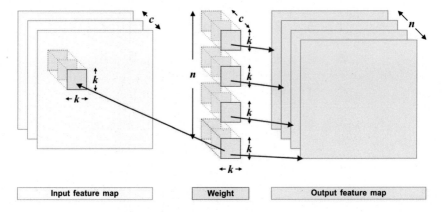

| Input feature map | Weight | Output feature map |

Figure 2.6 The diagram of convolution operation, where *c* is the number of input feature map channels, *n* is the number of convolutional kernels, and *k* × *k* is the size of a convolutional kernel.

tioned convolutional kernel, also known as a filter or weight. The weight window slides on the input feature map and computes the convolution with the feature map to obtain the output feature map. The filter can be shared, and only the feature map data in the filter window participate in the operation during each convolution computation. This is based on two considerations of image vision: first, only local neurons are important, and connections between neurons that are further apart can be ignored; second, patterns of the same picture may show any position of the image, and the same weight needs to be used for computation by sliding on the input data. The sparse connection and parameter sharing mechanism reduces the number of parameters of the model and improves the trainability of deep neural network.

In a convolutional layer, the size of the output feature map is determined by the convolutional kernel size, stride, and zero-padding. The stride is the value of the pixel that the convolutional kernel moves each time it slides. Zero-padding means that the edge of the input feature map is filled with 0, which controls the spatial size of the output data volume. It is worth noting that these three variables are all hyperparameters of a deep neural network model. Different from parameters that can be obtained through training (such as the weight and bias), hyperparameters are variables determined by experience, such as the convolutional kernel size and convolutional kernel depth mentioned here, as well as the model training learning rate and iteration hyperparameters to be mentioned later.

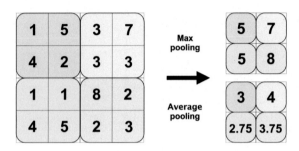

Figure 2.7 The illustration of two different types of pooling, max pooling and average pooling.

The pooling layer is a hidden layer used to abstract information in a deep neural network. Pooling is also a method to reduce the amount of computation of the model, which can increase the receptive field and reduce the difficulty and parameters of optimization. Fig. 2.7 shows two common pooling operations [10]. For each feature map channel, a window sliding operation is performed to realize max pooling (take the maximum value) or average pooling (take the average value) of data in the window to reduce the amount of data, prevent overfitting, and improve the generalization ability of the model. Generally, the pooling stride is greater than 1, which is used to reduce the scale of feature map. As shown in Fig. 2.7, the 4×4 feature map passes through a 2×2 pooling layer, whose stride is 2, and the output size is 2×2.

A convolutional neural network, as an important supporting technology of deep learning, promotes the development of artificial intelligence. Convolution operators can effectively extract spatial information and are widely used in the field of visual images, including image recognition [11], image segmentation [12], target detection [13], etc. In the model inference stage, the image data is input into the network, multilevel feature extraction is carried out through computation of multiple macromodules, and the prediction results of categories are output using a fully connected layer. In the model training stage, for a given input data, the error between the predicted result of a label and the real label is computed. Then the error gradient with respect to each parameter is computed by the back propagation algorithm. Finally, the parameters are updated by using the gradient descent algorithm. The above iterative steps are repeated for many times to gradually reduce the neural network prediction error until it converges. Compared with traditional feedforward neural networks, the convolutional neural network generally has better prediction accuracy and is one of the most important deep neural network structures.

2.2.2 Recurrent neural networks

Both the deep feedforward and convolutional neural networks mentioned above have a characteristic that their network structures are arranged in order, neurons in the lth layer receive only signals from neurons in the $(l-1)$th layer, and there is no feedback structure. However, in a particular task, to better capture the time-sequential features of the input vector, it is sometimes necessary to combine the sequential inputs. For example, in speech signal processing, if an exact translation of a sentence is required, then it is obviously impossible to translate each word separately. Instead, the words need to be connected together to form a sequence, and then the entire time-sequential sequence is processed. The recurrent neural network (RNN) [14] described in this section is a neural network structure that processes time-sequential data and has feedback.

RNN, originated in the 1980s and 1990s [15], is a recursive neural network that takes sequence data as input, adds feedback in the evolution direction of the sequence, and links all nodes in a chain. It is difficult for a traditional feedforward neural network to establish a time-dependent model, whereas RNN can integrate information from input unit and previous time node, allowing information to continue to function across the time node. This means that the network has a memory function, which is very useful in natural language processing, translation, speech recognition, and video processing.

Fig. 2.8 shows the basic structure of a standard RNN. On the left, there is a folded diagram, and on the right, there is the structure diagram expanded in chronological order. We can see that the loop body structure of RNN is located in the hidden layer. This network structure reveals the essence of RNN: the network information of the previous moment will act on that of the next moment, that is, the historical information of the previous moment will be connected to the neuron of the next moment through weights. As shown in the figure, in an RNN network, $\mathbf{x}$ represents an input, $\mathbf{h}$ represents a hidden layer unit, $\mathbf{o}$ represents an output, $\mathbf{y}$ represents a training label, t represents time, $\mathbf{U}$ is a parameter from the input layer to hidden layer, $\mathbf{V}$ is a parameter from the hidden layer to output layer, and $\mathbf{W}$ is a recurrent layer parameter. As we can see from the previous description, the performance of $\mathbf{h}$ at the moment of t is not only determined by the

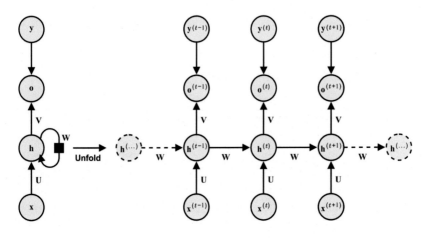

Figure 2.8 The schematic diagram of RNN, and its corresponding unfolded form.

input at that moment, but also influenced by the previous moment:

$$\mathbf{h}^{(t)} = \tanh(\mathbf{U}\mathbf{x}^{(t)} + \mathbf{W}\mathbf{h}^{(t-1)} + \mathbf{b}). \qquad (2.3)$$

The output at the moment of t is

$$\mathbf{o}^{(t)} = \mathbf{V}\mathbf{h}^{(t)} + \mathbf{c}. \qquad (2.4)$$

The final output predicted by the model is

$$\mathbf{y} = \sigma(\mathbf{o}^{(t)}). \qquad (2.5)$$

It is worth noting that for excessively long speech sequences, RNN only has short-term memory due to the problem of gradient vanishing during the training of back propagation model. Long short-term memory (LSTM) [16] and gate recurrent unit (GRU) [17] are two solutions to short-term memory of RNN, which introduce a gating mechanism to regulate information flow. Take the LSTM structure as an example. It contains a forget gate, an input gate, and an output gate, which are used to reserve or delete the incoming information and to record key information. LSTM performs well in long-term memory tasks, but the structure also leads to more parameters, making the training more difficult. Compared with LSTM, GRU with similar structure uses a single gate to complete the forget and selection information stages, reducing parameters while achieving the same performance as LSTM, which is widely used under the condition of limited computing resource and time cost.

2.3 Learning objectives and training process

2.3.1 Loss function

Deep learning model training and parameter estimation are generally based on the optimization of specific loss functions (or objective functions, collectively referred to as loss functions in this book). In model optimization theory, loss functions are a kind of functions that map the values of one or more variables to the real number field. For the training of neural network model, we use the loss function to measure the degree of inconsistency between the predicted value and the ground-truth label, which is a nonnegative real-valued function, so the loss function for all samples of the training set is usually expressed as

$$
\begin{aligned}
J(\boldsymbol{\theta}) &= \mathbb{E}_{(\mathbf{x},\mathbf{y})\sim P_{\text{data}}} \; \mathcal{L}(\mathbf{x}, \mathbf{y}; \boldsymbol{\theta}) \\
&= \mathbb{E}_{(\mathbf{x},\mathbf{y})\sim P_{\text{data}}} \; \mathcal{L}(f(\mathbf{x}; \boldsymbol{\theta}), \mathbf{y}),
\end{aligned}
\tag{2.6}
$$

where $\mathcal{L}$ is the loss function of each sample, $f(\mathbf{x}; \boldsymbol{\theta})$ is the output predicted by the model when $\mathbf{x}$ is the input, P_{data} is the empirical distribution, $\mathbb{E}$ represents expectation, $\mathbf{y}$ is the vector of all data labels, and $\boldsymbol{\theta}$ represents all parameters of the neural networks. The smaller the output of the loss function, the smaller the gap between the predicted value and the data label, and the better the performance of the model. Most importantly, the loss function is differentiable and can be used to solve optimization problems.

In the model training stage the predicted value is obtained through forward propagation after data is fed into the model, and then the loss function computes the difference between the predicted value and the data label, i.e., the loss value. The model updates the parameters by back propagation to reduce the loss value, so that the predicted value generated by the model is close to the ground-truth label of the data, so as to achieve the purpose of learning. In the following sections, we mainly introduce two loss functions in two classical prediction tasks, classification and regression.

The cross entropy loss function [18] is one of the most commonly used classification objective functions in current deep neural networks, which is a kind of loss functions based on probability distribution measurements. In information theory, entropy is used to describe the measurement of uncertainty. Cross entropy is originally used to estimate the average coding length, and in machine learning, it is used to evaluate the difference between the probability distribution obtained by current training and the real distribution. For a single sample, the cross entropy loss function takes the form

$$\mathcal{L} = -\sum_{k=1}^{C} y_k \log \hat{y}_k, \tag{2.7}$$

where C represents the number of output categories, $\hat{y}_k$ represents the kth output element ($k \in 1, 2, \ldots, C$) of the neural network, and the corresponding data label is y_k. If it is the corresponding category, then y_k is 1; otherwise, y_k is 0.

Different from the duality of data labels in a classification task (discrete type), each dimension of data labels in a regression task is a real number (successive type). In regression tasks the prediction error is frequently used to measure how close the predicted value of a model is to the data label. Assuming that the real label corresponding to the ith input feature $\mathbf{x}_i$ in a regression question is $\mathbf{y}_i = [y_{i1}, \ldots, y_{ik}, \ldots, y_{iM}]^T$, and M is the total dimension of label vector, the prediction error of the network regression predicted value $\hat{y}_{ik}$ and its real label y_{ik} in the kth dimension is

$$\mathcal{L}_{ik} = y_{ik} - \hat{y}_{ik}. \tag{2.8}$$

Loss functions frequently used in regression tasks are L1 [19] and L2 [20]. The L1 loss function for N samples is defined as

$$\mathcal{L} = \frac{1}{N} \sum_{i=1}^{N} \sum_{k=1}^{M} |\mathcal{L}_{ik}|. \tag{2.9}$$

There are many kinds of loss functions, including loss functions based on specific tasks, such as classification and regression tasks mentioned above, and loss functions based on distance measurement and probability distribution, for example, the mean square error loss function [21] and the L1 and L2 loss functions are based on distance measurement, whereas the cross entropy loss function and Softmax loss function [22] are based on probability distribution. The selection of a loss function needs to consider data features, and, in some cases, some regular terms should be added to improve the performance of the model.

2.3.2 Regularization

In model training, the loss value on the training sample can be continuously decreased by increasing the number of training iterations or adjusting hyperparameter settings. However, the prediction accuracy of the label of the training sample may keep improving, but the prediction accuracy of the label of the testing sample decreases instead of rising, which is called overfitting. Therefore the regularization method should be used to improve the generalization ability of the model and avoid overfitting.

Regularization is a method designed to reduce generalization errors, i.e., the errors of the model on testing samples, to correct models. In traditional machine learning algorithms, the generalization ability is mainly improved by limiting the complexity of the model. Generally speaking, the model complexity is linearly related to the data amount of weight parameters $\mathbf{W}$: the larger the data volume of $\mathbf{W}$, the greater the complexity, and the more complex the model. Therefore, to limit the complexity of the model, it is quite natural to reduce the number of weight parameters $\mathbf{W}$, that is, to make some elements in $\mathbf{W}$ be zero or limit the number of nonzero elements. Make the parameter θ of the neural network contain the weight coefficients of all neural network levels. The complexity of model parameters can be limited by adding a parameter penalty $\Omega(\theta)$ to the loss function. The regularized loss function is denoted as

$$\tilde{\mathcal{L}}(\mathbf{x}, \mathbf{y}; \theta) = \mathcal{L}(\mathbf{x}, \mathbf{y}; \theta) + \alpha \Omega(\theta), \tag{2.10}$$

where $\alpha \in [0, \infty)$ is the hyperparameter weighing the relative contribution of regularization term Ω and standard objective function $\mathcal{L}(\mathbf{x}, \mathbf{y}; \theta)$. Setting α to 0 indicates that there is no regularization, and the larger the α, the greater the corresponding regularization contribution.

By introducing regularization terms we hope to limit the number of nonzero elements in vector $\mathbf{W}$, so that the weight parameters are as small as possible and close to 0. The most frequently used regularization penalty is the L2 norm, which suppresses the weights of large values by applying an element-by-element squared penalty to all parameters. The L2 parameter norm penalty is also known as the weight decay [23], which is a regularization strategy that makes the weight closer to the origin by adding a regularization term $\Omega = \frac{1}{2}\|\mathbf{W}\|_2^2$ to the objective function.

2.3.3 Gradient-based optimization method

As mentioned earlier, model training is achieved by minimizing loss functions in machine learning. Under normal circumstances, the loss function is very complicated, and it is difficult to solve the analytic expression of minimum value. The gradient descent [24] is designed to solve this kind of problem. For ease of understanding, let us take an example and regard the process of solving the minimum value of a loss function as "standing somewhere on a slope to look for the lowest point". We do not know the exact location of the lowest point, the gradient descent strategy is to take a small step in the direction of downward slope, and after a long downward walk, there is a high probability that you will end up near the lowest point. We select the direction of downward slope to be the negative direction of the gradient, because the negative direction of the gradient at each point is the steepest downward direction of the function at that point. Deep neural networks usually use the gradient descent to update parameters, and by introduction of random, adjustment of learning rate, and other methods it is hoped that the networks can avoid falling into poor local minimum points and converge to better points. This is the traditional idea of gradient descent.

Stochastic gradient descent (SGD) is one of the most frequently used methods for updating parameters. In that method, the gradient of loss function with respect to parameters is computed by using a mini-batch of random sample data of the whole data set. SGD typically divides the whole data set into several small batches of sample data, then iterates the input and computes losses and gradients, and finally updates the parameters. Set the neural network parameter θ and collect a small batch of $\{\mathbf{x}_1, \mathbf{x}_2, \ldots, \mathbf{x}_N\}$ containing N samples from the training set, where $\mathbf{x}_i$ corresponds to the label $\mathbf{y}_i$. The following equations show the computation principle of gradient descent [25].

Gradient computation

$$\hat{\mathbf{g}} \leftarrow \frac{1}{m} \nabla_\theta \sum_i \mathcal{L}(f(\mathbf{x}_i; \boldsymbol{\theta}), \mathbf{y}_i). \qquad (2.11)$$

Application update

$$\boldsymbol{\theta} \leftarrow \boldsymbol{\theta} - \varepsilon \hat{\mathbf{g}}, \qquad (2.12)$$

where $\hat{\mathbf{g}}$ represents the gradient of the loss function with respect to parameter $\boldsymbol{\theta}$, and ε is called the learning rate, which is a hyperparameter to control the update stride of parameters. A too large learning rate will fluctuate near the minimum value but fail to converge, and a too little learning rate leads to spending more time for convergence, so the convergence speed is slow. The learning rate can be adjusted by experience or algorithms. For example, the learning process may be slower when a flat or high-curvature area is encountered. A momentum algorithm can be added to SGD to improve the convergence speed. At present, there are also adaptive algorithms such as Adaptive Moment Estimation (Adam) algorithm [26] and RMSProp algorithm [27], which can make an optimization from both the gradient and the learning rate to achieve good results.

In deep learning, gradient computation is complicated because of the large number of network layers and parameters. Back propagation algorithm [28] is widely used in gradient computation of neural network parameters. The principle of the back propagation algorithm is to compute the gradient of the loss function with respect to each weight parameter layer by layer through the chain rule. Then based on the chain rule, the reverse iteration is performed from the last layer, and the weight parameters of the model are updated at the end of each iteration. In the process of model training, weight parameters are constantly updated by inputting different batches of data until the loss function values converge to get a better parameter solution.

2.4 Computational complexity

From the perspective of complexity, two considerations should be taken into account when designing a CNN network. One is the amount of computation required by the network, and the other is the scale of the parameters of the model and the input and output features of each layer. The former determines the speed of network training or inferring, usually measured by time complexity, and the latter determines how much memory a computing device needs, usually measured by space complexity.

The time complexity of an algorithm is a function that describes the running time of an input algorithm of a given size. It can describe the trend of change in code execution time with the increase in data size. Generally speaking, the time complexity of the algorithm can be understood as the total time spent completing a set of specific algorithms. On a specific device the time is determined by the total amount of computation required by the execution of the algorithm. The frequently used units for the measurement of amount of computation of deep learning algorithms are required floating-point operations and FLOPS. Floating point operations per second (FLOPS) is a measure of computer performance, useful in fields of scientific computations that require floating-point calculations. For such cases, it is a more accurate measure than measuring instructions per second. At present, the total amount of computation of most convolutional neural networks can reach dozens or even hundreds of GigaFLOPs, such as the common convolutional neural network models MobileNet-V2 [29] and ResNet-50 [30], with a total amount of computation of 33.6 GFLOPs to 109.8 GFLOPs, which makes it difficult for neural networks deployed at the edge to complete real-time reasoning.

The space complexity refers to the amount of memory space required to solve an instance of the computational problem as a function of characteristics of the input, which is usually measured in units of computer memory. Inside a computer, information is stored, computed, and transmitted in binary form. The most basic units of storage are bits and bytes.

In convolutional neural networks the space complexity is mainly determined by the size of parameters at all layers. The parameters of the convolutional layer are mainly determined by the size and number of convolutional kernels, whereas the parameters of the fully connected layer are determined by the number of input neurons and output neurons. Take AlexNet [31], the champion model of 2012 ImageNet Image Classification Challenge, for example, which contains five convolutional layers with parameter sizes of 35 KB, 307 KB, 884 KB, 1.3 MB, and 442 KB, respectively, and three fully connected layers with parameter sizes of 37 MB, 16 MB, and 4 MB. The total size of parameters in AlexNet is about 60 MB, among which the fully connected structure undoubtedly increases the size of parameters, contributing 57 MB of parameters. Some CNN models that emerged after AlexNet performed better, but they were difficult to deploy on edge computing terminals due to their high space complexity.

References

[1] D. Svozil, V. Kvasnicka, J. Pospichal, Introduction to multi-layer feed-forward neural networks, Chemometrics and Intelligent Laboratory Systems 39 (1) (1997) 43–62.
[2] B.D. Ripley, Neural networks and related methods for classification, Journal of the Royal Statistical Society: Series B (Methodological) 56 (3) (1994) 409–437.
[3] R. Sylwester, A Celebration of Neurons: An Educator's Guide to the Human Brain, ERIC, 1995.
[4] A.N. Burkitt, A review of the integrate-and-fire neuron model: I. Homogeneous synaptic input, Biological Cybernetics 95 (1) (2006) 1–19.
[5] F. Agostinelli, M. Hoffman, P. Sadowski, P. Baldi, Learning activation functions to improve deep neural networks, arXiv:1412.6830 [abs].
[6] G. Huang, Y. Chen, H.A. Babri, Classification ability of single hidden layer feedforward neural networks, IEEE Transactions on Neural Networks 11 (3) (2000) 799–801.
[7] Y. Pang, M. Sun, X. Jiang, X. Li, Convolution in convolution for network in network, IEEE Transactions on Neural Networks and Learning Systems 29 (5) (2017) 1587–1597.
[8] W. Luo, Y. Li, R. Urtasun, R. Zemel, Understanding the effective receptive field in deep convolutional neural networks, in: Proceedings of International Conference on Neural Information Processing Systems, 2016, pp. 4905–4913.

[9] S. Albawi, T.A. Mohammed, S. Al-Zawi, Understanding of a convolutional neural network, in: Proceedings of International Conference on Engineering and Technology, 2017, pp. 1–6.

[10] D. Yu, H. Wang, P. Chen, Z. Wei, Mixed pooling for convolutional neural networks, in: Proceedings of International Conference on Rough Sets and Knowledge Technology, 2014.

[11] S. Hijazi, R. Kumar, C. Rowen, et al., Using convolutional neural networks for image recognition, Cadence Design Systems (2015) 1–12.

[12] H. Ajmal, S. Rehman, U. Farooq, Q.U. Ain, F. Riaz, A. Hassan, Convolutional neural network based image segmentation: a review, in: Proceedings of Pattern Recognition and Tracking XXIX, 2018.

[13] Z. Wang, J. Liu, A review of object detection based on convolutional neural network, in: Proceedings of Chinese Control Conference, 2017, pp. 11104–11109.

[14] Z.C. Lipton, A critical review of recurrent neural networks for sequence learning, arXiv:1506.00019 [abs].

[15] J.J. Hopfield, Neural networks and physical systems with emergent collective computational abilities, Proceedings of the National Academy of Sciences 79 (8) (1982) 2554–2558.

[16] S. Hochreiter, J. Schmidhuber, Long short-term memory, Neural Computation 9 (8) (1997) 1735–1780.

[17] R. Dey, F.M. Salem, Gate-variants of gated recurrent unit (GRU) neural networks, in: Proceedings of IEEE International Midwest Symposium on Circuits and Systems, 2017, pp. 1597–1600.

[18] D.M. Kline, V. Berardi, Revisiting squared-error and cross-entropy functions for training neural network classifiers, Neural Computing & Applications 14 (2005) 310–318.

[19] M.W. Schmidt, G. Fung, R. Rosales, Fast optimization methods for L1 regularization: A comparative study and two new approaches, in: Proceedings of European Conference on Machine Learning, 2007.

[20] P. Bühlmann, B. Yu, Boosting with the L2 loss: regression and classification, Journal of the American Statistical Association 98 (462) (2003) 324–339.

[21] S. Singh, D. Singh, S. Kumar, Modified mean square error algorithm with reduced cost of training and simulation time for character recognition in backpropagation neural network, in: Proceedings of International Conference on Frontiers in Intelligent Computing: Theory and Applications, 2013.

[22] W. Liu, Y. Wen, Z. Yu, M. Yang, Large-margin softmax loss for convolutional neural networks, arXiv:1612.02295 [abs].

[23] A. Krogh, J. Hertz, A simple weight decay can improve generalization, in: Proceedings of International Conference on Neural Information Processing Systems, 1991.

[24] E. Dogo, O. Afolabi, N. Nwulu, B. Twala, C. Aigbavboa, A comparative analysis of gradient descent-based optimization algorithms on convolutional neural networks, in: Proceedings of International Conference on Computational Techniques, Electronics and Mechanical Systems, 2018, pp. 92–99.

[25] Y. Bengio, I. Goodfellow, A. Courville, Deep Learning, vol. 1, MIT press, Massachusetts, USA, 2017.

[26] D.P. Kingma, J. Ba Adam, A method for stochastic optimization, arXiv:1412.6980 [abs].

[27] G. Hinton, N. Srivastava, K. Swersky, RMSProp: Divide the gradient by a running average of its recent magnitude, Neural Networks for Machine Learning, Coursera lecture 6e (2012) 13.

[28] D.E. Rumelhart, G.E. Hinton, R.J. Williams, Learning representations by back-propagating errors, Nature 323 (6088) (1986) 533–536.

[29] M. Sandler, A.G. Howard, M. Zhu, A. Zhmoginov, L.-C. Chen, MobileNetV2: Inverted residuals and linear bottlenecks, in: Proceedings of IEEE Conference on Computer Vision and Pattern Recognition, 2018.

[30] K. He, X. Zhang, S. Ren, J. Sun, Deep residual learning for image recognition, in: Proceedings of IEEE Conference on Computer Vision and Pattern Recognition, 2016.

[31] A. Krizhevsky, I. Sutskever, G.E. Hinton, ImageNet classification with deep convolutional neural networks, Communications of the ACM 60 (2012) 84–90.

PART 2

Model and algorithm

CHAPTER 3

Model design and compression

3.1 Background and challenges

Although convolutional neural networks have achieved good results in such fields as computer vision and natural language processing, they are daunting to many embedded device-based applications due to their massive parameters. At present, deep learning models require large amounts of computing resource and memory, often accompanied by huge energy consumption. Large models become the biggest bottleneck when we need to deploy models on terminal devices with limited computing resources for real-time inference. The training and reasoning of deep neural networks usually heavily rely on GPU with high computing ability. The huge scale of features and the deluge of model parameters also greatly increase the time. Take as an example AlexNet [1], a network containing 60 million parameters. It takes two to three days to train the entire model on the ImageNet data set using NVIDA K40. In fact, Denil et al. [9] have shown that deep neural networks are facing severe overparameterization, and a small subset of the parameters can completely reconstruct the remaining parameters. For example, ResNet-50 [10], which has 50 convolutional layers, requires more than 95 MB of storage memory and more than 3.8 billion floating-point multiplication operations to process images. After some redundant weights are discarded, the network still works as usual, but more than 75% of the parameters and 50% of the computation time can be saved. This indicates that there is huge redundancy in the parameters of the model, which reveals the feasibility of model compression.

In the field of deep neural network study, model compression and acceleration have received great attention from researchers, and great progress has been made in the past few years. Significant advances in intelligent wearable devices and AIoT in recent years have created unprecedented opportunities for researchers to address the fundamental challenges of deploying deep learning systems to portable devices with limited resources, such as memory, CPU, energy, and bandwidth. A highly efficient deep learning method can have a significant impact on distributed systems, embedded devices, and FPGAs for artificial intelligence. For the design and compression of highly efficient deep neural network models, in this chapter, we will first analyze

Deep Learning on Edge Computing Devices
https://doi.org/10.1016/B978-0-32-385783-3.00011-9

several categories of typical lightweight neural network models in recent years and then discuss model compression technology for neural networks, including model pruning and knowledge distillation.

3.2 Design of lightweight neural networks

The lightweight model aims to reduce model parameters and computational complexity from the aspect of network structure design while maintaining model performance, which is a hotspot of deep learning study. With the same accuracy, a smaller CNN architecture will consume fewer resources and be more suitable for deployment on embedded edge terminal devices with limited memory and computing resources. In this section, we mainly focus on the design of network structure and give a brief description of lightweight networks, including the following types of lightweight models.

3.2.1 SqueezeNet

Researchers at UC Berkeley and Stanford first proposed a small CNN architecture called SqueezeNet in 2016 [11], which was one of the early studies focusing on lightweight networks. They reduced the number of network parameters to less than 0.5 MB, 510 times smaller than that of AlexNet, but with the same accuracy as AlexNet. To do this, they used three strategies to reduce the number of parameters and maintain accuracy.

- Strategy 1: Replace the 3×3 convolution with the 1×1 convolution, so that the number of parameters for a convolutional kernel can be reduced by 9 times.
- Strategy 2: Reduce the number of input channels for the 3×3 filter via squeeze layer.
- Strategy 3: Delay downsampling. The higher the number of the layer, the larger the feature map, which is conducive to improving the accuracy of the model.

The basic unit in SqueezeNet is called Fire Module. A Fire Module consists of a Squeeze layer and an Expand layer, as shown in Fig. 3.1. Squeeze layer only uses a 1×1 convolutional kernel to realize strategy 1, whereas Expand Layer uses the convolutional combination of 1×1 and 3×3. There are three adjustable parameters in the Module, namely, the number of 1×1 convolutional kernels in Squeeze layer s_1, the number of 1×1 convolutional kernels in Expand layer e_1 and the number of 3×3

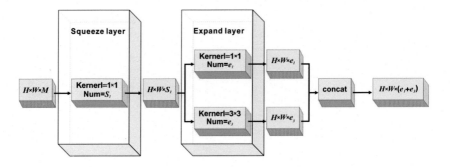

Figure 3.1 The structure of Fire Module [11].

convolutional kernels in Expand layer e_3. Let $s_1 < e_1 + e_3$ to limit the number of input channels for 3×3 convolution to realize strategy 2. Use the ReLU function between Squeeze layer and Expand layer for activation.

SqueezeNet is composed of several Fire Modules combined with a pooling layer. A complete SqueezeNet network has 10 layers, of which the first layer is a convolutional layer, and the second to ninth layers are Fire Modules, where the number of filters in Fire Module increases layer by layer. The convolutional layer at the tenth layer is followed by a global AvgPool layer. Finally, the classification results are output by the softmax function. The first, fourth, and eighth layers are followed by a downsampling module using the MaxPool approach. Note that there is no fully connected layer in the network structure of SqueezeNet. Experimental results show that both Top-1 and Top-5 performances of SqueezeNet are better than those of AlexNet [1], but the model size is reduced from 240 MB to 4.8 MB, making it possible to deploy SqueezeNet on embedded edge devices. SqueezeNet has fewer parameters, but deeper network has led to an increase in test time. However, SqueezeNet pioneered the study of lightweight models, and then more high-performance models emerged in the related field.

3.2.2 MobileNet

In 2017, researchers at Google implemented a new streamlined network architecture based on depthwise separable convolution, which was called MobileNet [12]. The depthwise separable convolution can be broken down into two smaller convolution operations, depthwise and pointwise convolutions, as shown in Fig. 3.2. The difference between depthwise and standard convolutions lies in that, for standard convolution, its convolutional kernel

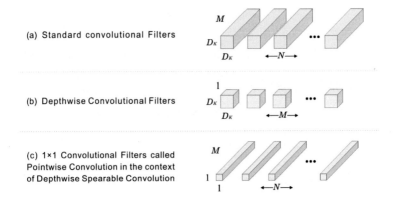

(a) Standard convolutional Filters

(b) Depthwise Convolutional Filters

(c) 1×1 Convolutional Filters called Pointwise Convolution in the context of Depthwise Spearable Convolution

Figure 3.2 Depthwise and pointwise convolutions [12].

acts on all input channels. The depthwise convolution is an operation at the depth level, in which each convolutional kernel acts on only one input channel. This approach is also called the group convolution. However, this also results in too few feature map dimensions due to too few channels, and pointwise convolution refers to the use of multiple 1×1 convolutional kernels to raise the dimension of the feature map while exchanging information among feature maps.

The depthwise separable convolution refers to the convolution of different input channels using 3×3 depthwise convolution, followed by the combination of output by 1×1 pointwise convolution, as shown in Fig. 3.3. Note that both depthwise and pointwise convolutions are followed by batch normalization BatchNorm and activation function ReLU. Although the result of depthwise separable convolution is the same as that of ordinary convolution, the number of parameters and the amount of computation are reduced to about one-eighth of those of the standard convolution computation.

MobileNetV1 [12] contains a total of 28 layers, among which 13 are depthwise separable convolutional layers. For some of depthwise convolutions, the stride is set to 2 for downsampling, and the prediction results are finally output through the softmax layer. MobileNet also introduces two hyperparameters, the width and resolution multipliers, to reduce the complexity of the model. For a depthwise separable convolutional layer, the numbers of input and output channels are multiplied by the width multiplier to evenly thin the network, whereas the resolution multiplier can reduce resource consumption by reducing the resolution.

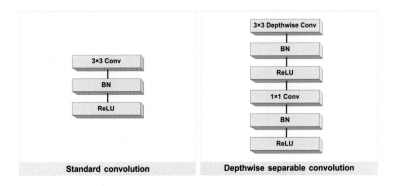

Figure 3.3 Comparison of standard and depthwise separable convolutions.

Experiments show that MobileNetV1 has less amount of computation than GoogleNet [13] but better classification performance. VGG-16 [14] performs 30 times more computation to achieve only 1% higher accuracy than MoblieNetV1. However, since it is easy to result in information loss when ReLU computation is performed on low dimensions, the author proposed an improved MobileNetV2 structure [15]. Compared with MobileNetV1, MobileNetV2 has a pointwise convolution that is added before the depthwise convolution, which aims to enhance feature dimension, and at the same time, the ReLU activation function after the second pointwise convolution is removed, because the main function of the second pointwise convolution is to reduce the dimension.

The effectiveness of MobileNet has been proven in a wide range of applications, with good performance in such areas as target detection and face recognition. However, MoblieNet spends 95% of the computation time and 75% of the parameters on 1 × 1 convolution, and the network structure needs to be further improved.

3.2.3 ShuffleNet

As mentioned above, the 1 × 1 pointwise convolution increases the computational complexity of the network, whereas the group convolution causes information blocking between channels. To solve these problems, researchers at Megvii proposed channel shuffle, an operation to assist in information flow and enhance feature mapping, based on which they established a highly efficient network architecture, ShuffleNet [16].

The traditional depthwise separable convolution consists of a 3 × 3 depthwise convolution and 1 × 1 pointwise convolutions. However, a large

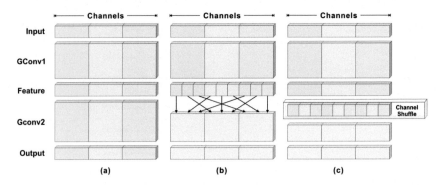

Figure 3.4 Illustration of channel shuffle with two stacked group convolutions [16]. GConv stands for group convolution.

number of 1×1 pointwise convolutions leads to poor direct information communication of convolutions, resulting in loss of accuracy. Because each channel can only correspond to a limited convolutional kernel, the expressive ability to output the feature set is greatly reduced. This 1×1 convolutional structure is also known as bottleneck. To solve this problem, ShuffleNet uses channel shuffle. As shown in Fig. 3.4, the process of channel shuffle is equivalent to reorganizing feature maps after group convolution and grouping the feature maps after shuffling the orders to ensure information flow between different groups.

The basic unit of ShuffleNet is improved on the basis of a residual unit. This basic residual unit is shown in Fig. 3.5(a), that is, 1×1 convolution is performed first, then 3×3 depthwise convolution is performed to reduce the amount of computation, and finally the input is directly added to the output via 1×1 convolution, which is similar to the improved depthwise separable convolutional layer of MobileNetV2. After the introduction of channel shuffle, the module is introduced between the first pointwise convolution and depthwise convolution to form the basic structure of ShuffleNet, as shown in Fig. 3.5(b). For each residual unit, it is only needed to add channel shuffle after the first pointwise convolution. When stride $= 2$, the input does not match the output, and the solution is to perform the average pooling with stride $= 2$ on the original input and then to connect the feature map to the output, as shown in Fig. 3.5(c).

Based on the basic unit designed above, the overall structure of ShuffleNet network is as follows: The input image first passes through the ordinary convolutional layer and max pooling layer, and then continuously passes through three Stage structures. Each Stage is formed by several

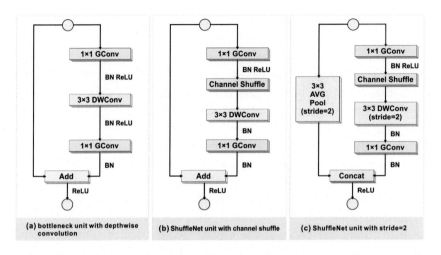

(a) bottleneck unit with depthwise convolution

(b) ShuffleNet unit with channel shuffle

(c) ShuffleNet unit with stride=2

Figure 3.5 The basic unit of ShuffleNet [16].

stacked ShuffleNet basic units, among which the first basic unit has a stride of 2, as shown in Fig. 3.5(c), and the basic units that follow all have a stride of 1, as shown in Fig. 3.5(b). When the three Stages are completed, the global pool is used to reduce the size of feature map to 1×1, and the prediction results are finally output through the softmax layer. ShuffleNet can use more generous feature maps under the same limitation on computing resources. Experiments show that within a certain range, the more the groups, the stronger the classification ability of ShuffleNet, but too many groups can also cause network saturation and even accuracy degradation.

3.2.4 EfficientNet

Empirically, to improve the accuracy and speed of network, the dimensions of width, depth, and resolution need to be balanced. So how do we balance these three dimensions at the same time to get the best network architecture under constraints? The previous methods were basically to adjust one or two of these three dimensions to determine the optimal network structure through experiments. It is clear that the optimal network structure obtained manually is likely to be locally optimal. Therefore Tan et al. [17] studied the model scaling and proposed EfficientNet, which balanced these three dimensions simultaneously through neural network architecture search (NAS) to find the optimal network architecture.

The model scaling is as shown in Fig. 3.6, and the compound scaling is determined primarily by three dimensions, including width, depth, and resolution, among which (a) is a baseline network architecture, (b), (c), and (d) illustrate the scaling of width, depth, and resolution, respectively, and (e) illustrates the compound scaling of width, depth, and resolution. For example, Fig. 3.6(b) can be interpreted as enlargement of width by 2 times. Fig. 3.6(c) can be interpreted as enlargement of depth by 2 times. Fig. 3.6(d) can be interpreted as enlargement of resolution by 2 times, and the scaling of all convolutional layers is consistent.

EfficientNet first determines that the search parameters are the dimensions of width, depth, and resolution, and the goal is to search out a set of optimal solutions of these three parameters and apply them to all the convolutional layers. Due to limited computing resources, NAS is actually a multiobjective optimization problem with constraints. The author points out that if only one dimension is scaled, then the accuracy of the model will soon become saturated, because width, depth, and resolution are interrelated. The EfficientNet model is constructed in two main steps: first, the baseline model Efficient-B0 is generated using the reinforcement learning method, and then these three interrelated dimensions are scaled simultaneously using the compound scaling method. The optimization model is shown as follows:

$$depth : d = \alpha^{\phi}, \qquad (3.1)$$
$$width : w = \beta^{\phi},$$
$$resolution : r = \gamma^{\phi},$$
$$s.t. \quad \alpha \cdot \beta^2 \cdot \gamma^2 \approx 2,$$
$$\alpha \geq 1, \beta \geq 1, \gamma \geq 1,$$

where the compound parameter ϕ is used to control the overall model scaling under resource constraints, and α, β, and γ specify how to allocate these resources to width, depth, and resolution, respectively. The search strategy is to set ϕ to 1 and then obtain three optimal scaling coefficients α, β, and γ through a small grid search. Then α, β, and γ are fixed, and ϕ is scaled to obtain a series of models from Efficient-B1 to Efficient-B7.

However, there are some problems with EfficientNet, for example, training on larger images is slower, and since depthwise separable convolution has fewer parameters than ordinary convolution, more variables are saved, resulting in slower training. Therefore Training-Aware NAS was proposed for EfficientNetV2 [18], which uses Fused Mbconv in the search space to combine 3×3 depthwise separable convolution and 1×1 convolution of Mbconv into an ordinary 3×3 convolution to reduce the search

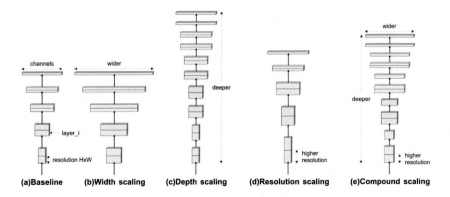

Figure 3.6 The illustration of model scaling [17].

Table 3.1 The comparison of EfficientNet and EfficientNetV2 [18].

	EfficientNet	EfficientNetV2
Search Space	MBconv	MBconv, Fused MBconv
Search Strategy	Grid search	Random search
Performance Evaluation Strategy	FLOPS	Time, Parameter

space. Moreover, since the search space is reduced, search can be done using random search. Comparison of EfficientNet and EfficientNetV2 is shown in Table 3.1. Experiments have shown that compared with ResNet [10], DenseNet [19], Inception [13], and NASNet [20], EfficientNet achieves higher accuracy with fewer parameters.

3.3 Model compression

With rapid development of deep learning, more and more parameters are used in deep neural network model. Models with outstanding results in ImageNet Challenge [1] all have massive parameters, such as the ResNet-50 model [10], which has 50 million parameters, and the VGG-16 model [14], which has 130 million parameters. In addition, the number of parameters of the GPT model [21] in the field of natural language processing has expanded from 110 million in GPT1 to 175 billion in GPT3. Large models with massive parameters not only consume a lot of resources during training, but also prevent the deployment to mobile devices such as mobile phones and robots. In the context of Artificial Intelligence & Internet of Things (AIoT), the need for model compression becomes more urgent. Only by reducing the parameters of the model, miniaturizing the model structure, and reducing the amount of computation of neural network model inference the model can be deployed on terminal devices.

Model compression refers to the transformation of a large and complex model into a small streamlined model that can achieve performance similar to that of the large model. At present, technology related to model compression mainly includes, but not limited to, the following methods.

- Low-rank decomposition [22,23]: The convolutional kernel of a convolutional neural network is a 4D tensor, and this weight matrix is often dense and low-rank, with great redundancy information. By means of low-rank decomposition the dense matrix can be broken down into several small-scale matrices to achieve model compression. However, the cost of matrix decomposition is high, the layer-by-layer decomposition of convolutional kernel matrix is not conducive to the compression of global parameters, and the 1×1 small convolutional kernel is more often used in the network now, which is not conducive to the low-rank decomposition method, and it is difficult to achieve the compression of the model.

- Model Pruning [2–8,24–26]: On the basis of pretrained large model, design evaluation criteria for the importance of network parameters to measure their importance and remove some unimportant parameters to speed up the network and improve the generalization ability.

- Knowledge distillation [27–29]: In general, large models tend to be a single complex network or a collection of several networks, with good performance and generalization ability, whereas small models have limited expressive ability because of the small scale of the network. Therefore the knowledge learned by large models can be used to guide the training of small models, so that the small models have the same performance as the large models, but the number of parameters is greatly reduced, so as to achieve model compression, that is, the knowledge of pretrained large teacher models is refined into lightweight student models.

- Parameter quantification [30,31]: Reduce the space and computational overhead of network parameters by sacrificing some accuracy. For example, a typical 32-bit floating-point network parameter is represented by a lower bit width (1 bit, 2 bits, 8 bits, 16 bits), including weight, activation value, gradient, and error. Parameter quantification will lead to loss of some information, resulting in performance degradation of the final model, but it also has obvious advantages: (1) parameter storage

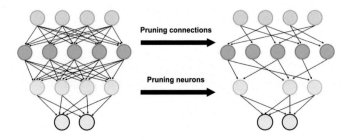

Figure 3.7 The illustration of model pruning [26].

space and memory footprint can be significantly reduced, and (2) computation can be accelerated, and device power consumption can be lowered.

Next, we will introduce model pruning and knowledge distillation and describe in detail the parameter quantification in the following chapters.

3.3.1 Model pruning

Model pruning is a classic technique in the field of model compression, as shown in Fig. 3.7. As mentioned above, in deep neural networks, many parameters are redundant and have little effect on error reduction and model generalization during training, so removing these parameters will not have a significant impact on network performance. Google conducted experiments on the Inception V3 model to explore the relationship between parameter sparsity and performance [32]. Experiments showed that the performance of the model was almost unchanged when the sparsity was 50%, and the classification accuracy on ImageNet only decreased by 2% when the sparsity was 87.5%. Similarly, they found that, on the small model MobileNet, the sparse wide MobileNet model performed significantly better than the nonsparse narrow MobileNet model with the same number of parameters. These experiments undoubtedly show the necessity and feasibility of model pruning. Pruning can not only reduce the model complexity, but also effectively prevent overfitting and improve the generalization ability of the model.

The model pruning can be performed either during training or after training. For convolutional neural networks, model pruning can be roughly divided into two categories, weight pruning [26] and filter pruning [25]. Weight pruning means that all weight connections below a certain threshold will be removed. Filter pruning means that the importance of filters is

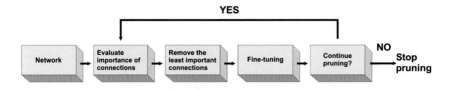

Figure 3.8 The procedure of weight pruning.

sorted in the convolutional neural network and those unimportant filters
are removed. The importance of filters can be computed by the L1 and L2
norms. Although the algorithmic details of various pruning schemes vary,
the basic frameworks used are similar. There are two kinds of model pruning algorithms. One is performing pruning according to the importance
of parameters on the basis of pretraining model, and then fine-tuning the
training; the other is performing sparse regularization constraints on the
model and performing the model pruning during training.

Song Han et al. [26] first proposed a method for completely removing weight connections below a certain threshold, because too low weight
value means that the connection is less important. Their pruning strategy
mainly includes four steps.

•   The first step is training an initial model, obtaining an intensive net-
    work model;
•   The second step is measuring the importance of weight connections;
•   The third step is deleting all the connections with the weight below
    the threshold from the network to convert the intensive network to a
    sparse network;
•   The fourth step is to fine-tuning the network and learning the final
    weight of the sparse connection.

Among these steps, the second, third, and fourth steps can be iterated
repeatedly to obtain the optimal model. The specific process is shown in
Fig. 3.8. The key steps are: (1) how to measure the importance of the
connection, and (2) how to restore the performance of the model after
pruning.

Experimental results show that their method reduces the number of
AlexNet parameters by 9 times and that of VGG-16 parameters by 13
times without any loss of accuracy. However, this pruning algorithm has
the defect that irregular network distribution after pruning leads to frequent
switching between CPU cache and memory, which restricts the acceleration effect. Moreover, most of the weight parameters for pruning are from

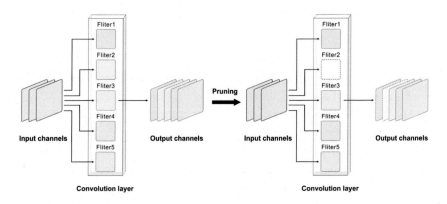

Figure 3.9 The illustration of filter pruning.

the fully connected layer, but the fully connected layer contributes very little to the total floating-point operation, so the calculation time may not be significantly reduced.

In view of the problems of the weight pruning method, Li et al. [25] tried to prune directly at the level of filter (convolutional kernel), that is, to remove the feature maps of filters and their connections from the network. In contrast to weight pruning, this approach does not result in a sparse connection mode. It is noted that there is obvious redundancy between the convolution kernel and the feature map in convolutional layer and the convolutional layer takes up most of the floating-point computation in the neural network, so the goal of acceleration can be directly achieved by reducing the number of matrix multiplications. Filter pruning is shown in Fig. 3.9. When a convolutional kernel of a convolutional layer is pruned out, the corresponding feature map disappears, and the reduction of output channels leads to the reduction of the dimension of the convolutional channel of the next layer. The core of the algorithm is determining the importance of the filters. The strategy adopted by them is measuring the importance of each filter by the weight, i.e., for each filter, all the corresponding weight absolute values are summed (i.e., L1 norm), and then the filter with the minimum sorting result value and its associated connections and channels are pruned out. The specific pruning process is as follows:

- Training an initial model;
- Calculating the sum of weight absolute values of all the convolutional kernels and then carrying out sorting;
- Pruning out convolutional kernels with the minimum sum of weight absolute values and the corresponding feature maps and removing ker-

nels related to the pruned feature maps from the next convolutional layer;
- Finally, creating a new kernel matrix for the ith and $(i+1)$th layers and copying the remaining kernel weights into the new model;
- Fine-tuning the retrained network.

For the aforementioned weight pruning, iterative training and loss compensation are carried out layer by layer. However, for the filters, pruning and retaining layer by layer will take a lot of time, so it is necessary to simultaneously prune out filters of multiple layers. At the experimental stage, the number of floating-point operations of VGG-16 was reduced by 34.2%, the parameters were reduced by 64.0%, and the error rate was reduced.

The filter pruning algorithm is based on the weights to measure its contribution to the network, but in fact, in the case of adopting a large compression ratio, directly discarding these weights will cause irreversible damage to the accuracy of the network. The weight pruning and filter pruning mentioned above are both measured at the level of weight. There are other methods to achieve model pruning, such as data-driven pruning [33,34].

3.3.2 Knowledge distillation

In the context of model compression, we hope to deploy models with less computing resource demands to edge devices, but it is difficult to train a small model from scratch to achieve the powerful learning ability and accuracy of a large model (overparameterized model). Although most people think that the number of parameters of a model determines the amount of knowledge that the model can capture, in fact, the relationship between the number of parameters of the model and the amount of captured knowledge presents a curve that is close to the gradual decrease of marginal revenue. Therefore one idea is to transfer the knowledge learned by a complex model to a small compact model through certain technical means so that the small model can achieve performance similar to a large model. The technology of Knowledge Distillation is based on this idea of transfer learning.

The necessity of Knowledge Distillation is mainly reflected in three points.
- The first is the correlation between model performance and scale. In general, driven by the same data set, a large model can achieve better performance than a small model, which is also the reason why the

layer of the deep neural network is getting deeper and deeper and the parameter scale is getting larger and larger.

- The second is the limited scale of data. Some data sets involving user privacy information are usually very expensive, and it is often impossible to support training a network from scratch. In this case, it is necessary to pretrain a general model on large data sets, because the underlying knowledge of data can be extracted by pretraining the model, and these underlying details are generic.
- The third is the actual demand. In some actual scenes (vertical fields) where only specific categories are involved, it makes more sense and performs better to transfer the knowledge from the general model pretrained on large data sets (such as ImageNet, which contains 1000 categories) directly to a small model than to train a small model from scratch.

The classical knowledge distillation algorithm is a kind of "Teacher–Student" models [35], wherein "Teacher" is a knowledge exporter, that is, the aforementioned complex model or a model set composed of several separately trained models, which is called "NET-T" hereinafter; and "Student" is a knowledge receiver, corresponding to a kind of small models, which is called "Net-S" hereinafter. The knowledge distillation process is mainly divided into three stages: firstly, using a complete data set to train Net-T on a GPU with high computing performance; secondly, establishing a corresponding relation between Net-S and Net-T; and finally, deploying Net-S that has gained generalization ability into the applications. Knowledge distillation can be divided into three categories according to the types of transferred knowledge [36]: response-based transfer [27,37–39], feature-based transfer [25,40–42], and relation-based transfer [29].

The most classical algorithm in response-based transfer was proposed by Hinton et al. [27], who regarded the probability output of the softmax function as a kind of valuable knowledge and hoped to use it as the matching target to make output distributions of Net-S and Net-T sufficiently close. However, the hard target adopted by traditional machine learning algorithms directly takes the maximum value of the Softmax classification probability as the model prediction label and ignores labels of the other probabilities, which may reduce the generalization ability of distillation models. Therefore, Hinton et al. proposed a concept of soft target, which improved the original function by introducing a hyperparameter T to control the entropy distribution of the prediction probability. The higher the T, the smoother the prediction probability distribution, and the

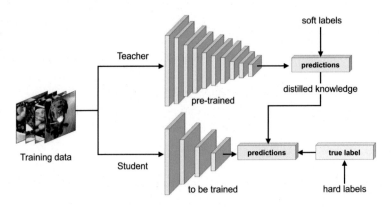

Figure 3.10 The illustration of output transfer-based knowledge distillation [27].

information carried by negative labels will be relatively amplified, so model training will pay more attention to the negative labels. The improved function, which is called the softmax-T function, has the form

$$q_i = \frac{\exp(z_i/T)}{\sum_j \exp(z_j/T)}. \tag{3.2}$$

Based on the pretrained teacher model Net-T and a student model Net-S to be trained, the distillation process is shown in Fig. 3.10.

- First, the training data set is simultaneously input to Net-T and Net-S at high temperature of $T = t$, and the output of the softmax-T function of Net-T and Net-S constitutes a cross entropy, which is taken as the first part $\mathcal{L}_{\text{soft}}$ of the loss function.
- Then the output of the softmax function of Net-S is taken as the second part $\mathcal{L}_{\text{hard}}$ of the loss function at normal temperature of $T = 1$.
- The total loss function $\mathcal{L}$ is composed of $\mathcal{L}_{\text{soft}}$ and $\mathcal{L}_{\text{hard}}$, and Net-S is trained with $\mathcal{L}$ as the loss function of Net-S.

Hinton pointed out through experiments that knowledge distillation enables the student model to acquire the knowledge of the teacher model so as to improve the effect of small models. This approach proposed by Hinton et al. has had profound influence on subsequent studies on knowledge distillation, and some improved forms for output transfer have also been proposed. For example, Ying Zhang et al. [37] proposed a Mutual Learning model for Net-S to learn from and guide each other in the training process. The classical distillation algorithm is a one-way channel that transfers knowledge from Net-T to Net-S, while Mutual Learning makes

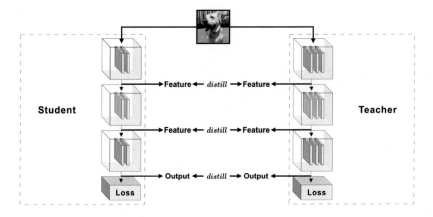

Figure 3.11 The illustration of featuret transfer based knowledge distillation.

the loss function of each Net-S composed of traditional supervised learning loss and imitation loss, and requires the prediction probabilities of Net-S to be consistent.

The knowledge distillation method based on output transfer is difficult to control the learning of intermediate detail features in the student model and will lead to unstable training. A more intuitive approach is to impose constraints on the intermediate features of the Net-T model and the Net-S model to ensure that the Net-S model can inherit all the knowledge of Net-T as accurately as possible. Such distillation is called feature transfer. Instead of directly taking the output of softmax as the target distillation to a small model, feature transfer emphasizes Net-S to learn the intermediate layer of Net-T network structure, that is, knowledge distillation is carried out simultaneously at the intermediate feature level and the output end, as shown in Fig. 3.11.

Output transfer has taken into account that Net-S has a smaller number of parameters than Net-T, but for Net-S with more layers and fewer neurons per layer than Net-T (this structure is called thin deep network), Hinton's method still needs to be expanded. Therefore Romero et al. [28] proposed a method for training thin deep network. By introducing a Net-T hidden layer output variable Hints for guiding the learning process of Net-S, the hidden layer of Net-S can learn the predictive output of the Net-T hidden layer. Net-S in this distillation mode is called FitNet.

The whole training process is divided into two stages, as shown in Fig. 3.12. The weight of an intermediate layer of the Net-T model is denoted as $\mathbf{W}_H$, indicating guiding, and the weight of an intermediate layer

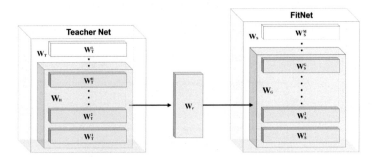

Figure 3.12 Illustration of FitNet knowledge distillation [28].

of the Net-S model is denoted as $\mathbf{W}_G$, indicating being guided. The first stage is matching the features from $\mathbf{W}_H$ and $\mathbf{W}_G$ of the intermediate layer. Since the output sizes of the two features are different, a mapping function $\mathbf{W}_r$ is used to achieve the size matching, and then the knowledge distillation of the features of the intermediate layer is realized by minimizing the difference between $\mathbf{W}_H$ and $\mathbf{W}_G$. At this stage the parameters of the first g layers of FitNet are trained by the guidance of the parameters of the first h layers of Net-T. The second stage is the same as the above output transfer, and the parameters $\mathbf{W}_S$ and $\mathbf{W}_G$ of all the layers of Net-S are obtained by training.

Experimental results show that the feature transfer method can provide more knowledge of the teacher model and improve the generalization ability of the student model better than the output transfer method. Moreover, FitNets, as a model compression algorithm, can strike an excellent balance between speed and accuracy, and the model performance decreases by only 1.3% under the condition of reducing parameters by 36 times. However, it is worth noting that the hint-based hidden layer feature mapping is actually a class of regularization representation, so the deeper the number of the $\mathbf{W}_G$ layer is set, the more likely FitNets is to be affected by excessive regularization. Other studies on feature transfer also start from the hidden layer, for example, the feature maps output by hidden layers of convolutional neural networks are transferred to Net-S, and the difference between the feature maps in Net-T and Net-S is calculated and reduced [40].

References

[1] A. Krizhevsky, I. Sutskever, G.E. Hinton, ImageNet classification with deep convolutional neural networks, Communications of the ACM 60 (2012) 84–90.

[2] H. Yang, S. Gui, Y. Zhu, J. Liu, Automatic neural network compression by sparsity-quantization joint learning: A constrained optimization-based approach, in: Proceedings of the IEEE Conference on Computer Vision and Pattern Recognition, 2020.

[3] Y. Guo, H. Yuan, J. Tan, Z. Wang, S. Yang, J. Liu, GDP: stabilized neural net-work pruning via gates with differentiable polarization, in: International Conference on Computer Vision, 2021.

[4] X. Ding, G. Ding, X. Zhou, Y. Guo, J. Han, J. Liu, Global sparse momentum SGD for pruning very deep neural networks, Neural Information Processing Systems (2019).

[5] J. Shen, H. Wang, S. Gui, J. Tan, Z. Wang, J. Liu, UMEC: Unified model and embedding compression for efficient recommendation systems, in: International Conference on Learning Representations, 2021.

[6] H. Yang, Y. Zhu, J. Liu, ECC: Platform-independent energy-constrained deep neural network compression via a bilinear regression model, in: Proceedings of the IEEE Conference on Computer Vision and Pattern Recognition, 2019, pp. 11206–11215.

[7] H. Wang, S. Gui, H. Yang, H. Yang, J. Liu, Z. Wang, GAN slimming: all-in-one GAN compression by a unified optimization framework, in: European Conference on Computer Vision, Springer, Cham, 2020, pp. 54–73.

[8] S. Gui, H. Wang, H. Yang, C. Yu, Z. Wang, J. Liu, Model compression with adversarial robustness: A unified optimization framework, Advances in Neural Information Processing Systems (2019) 1285–1296.

[9] M. Denil, B. Shakibi, L. Dinh, M. Ranzato, N.D. Freitas, Predicting parameters in deep learning, in: Proceedings of International Conference on Neural Information Processing Systems, 2013.

[10] K. He, X. Zhang, S. Ren, J. Sun, Deep residual learning for image recognition, in: Proceedings of IEEE Conference on Computer Vision and Pattern Recognition, 2016.

[11] F.N. Iandola, M. Moskewicz, K. Ashraf, S. Han, W. Dally, K. Keutzer, SqueezeNet: AlexNet-level accuracy with 50× fewer parameters and <1 MB model size, arXiv: 1602.07360 [abs].

[12] A.G. Howard, M. Zhu, B. Chen, D. Kalenichenko, W. Wang, T. Weyand, M. Andreetto, H. Adam, MobileNets: Efficient convolutional neural networks for mobile vision applications, arXiv:1704.04861 [abs].

[13] C. Szegedy, W. Liu, Y. Jia, P. Sermanet, S.E. Reed, D. Anguelov, D. Erhan, V. Vanhoucke, A. Rabinovich, Going deeper with convolutions, in: Proceedings of IEEE Conference on Computer Vision and Pattern Recognition, 2015.

[14] K. Simonyan, A. Zisserman, Very deep convolutional networks for large-scale image recognition, arXiv:1409.1556 [abs].

[15] M. Sandler, A.G. Howard, M. Zhu, A. Zhmoginov, L.-C. Chen, MobileNetV2: Inverted residuals and linear bottlenecks, in: Proceedings of IEEE Conference on Computer Vision and Pattern Recognition, 2018.

[16] X. Zhang, X. Zhou, M. Lin, J. Sun, ShuffleNet: An extremely efficient convolutional neural network for mobile devices, in: Proceedings of the IEEE Conference on Computer Vision and Pattern Recognition, 2018.

[17] M. Tan, Q. Le, EfficientNet: Rethinking model scaling for convolutional neural networks, in: Proceedings of International Conference on Machine Learning, 2019.

[18] Q.V. Tan, Mingxingand Le, EfficientNetV2: Smaller models and faster training, arXiv: 2104.00298 [abs].

[19] D. Singh, V. Kumar, M. Kaur, Densely connected convolutional networks-based COVID-19 screening model, Applied Intelligence (2021) 1–8.

[20] B. Zoph, V. Vasudevan, J. Shlens, Q.V. Le, Learning transferable architectures for scalable image recognition, in: Proceedings of IEEE Conference on Computer Vision and Pattern Recognition, 2018.

[21] A. Radford, K. Narasimhan, T. Salimans, I. Sutskever, Improving language under-standing by generative pre-training, Available: https://www.cs.ubc.ca/~amuham01/LING530/papers/radford2018improving.pdf, 2018.

[22] V. Sindhwani, T. Sainath, S. Kumar, Structured transforms for small-footprint deep learning, in: Proceedings of International Conference on Neural Information Process-ing Systems, 2015.

[23] E.L. Denton, W. Zaremba, J. Bruna, Y. LeCun, R. Fergus, Exploiting linear structure within convolutional networks for efficient evaluation, in: Proceedings of Conference and Workshop on Neural Information Processing Systems, 2014.

[24] S. Srinivas, R.V. Babu, Data-free parameter pruning for deep neural networks, in: Proceedings of British Machine Vision Conference, 2015.

[25] H. Li, A. Kadav, I. Durdanovic, H. Samet, H. Graf, Pruning filters for efficient Con-vNets, arXiv:1608.08710 [abs].

[26] S. Han, J. Pool, J. Tran, W. Dally, Learning both weights and connections for efficient neural network, arXiv:1506.02626 [abs].

[27] G.E. Hinton, O. Vinyals, J. Dean, Distilling the knowledge in a neural network, arXiv:1503.02531 [abs].

[28] A. Romero, N. Ballas, S. Kahou, A. Chassang, C. Gatta, Y. Bengio, FitNets: Hints for thin deep nets, arXiv:1412.6550 [abs].

[29] Y. Liu, J. Cao, B. Li, C. Yuan, W. Hu, Y. Li, Y.-f. Duan, Knowledge distillation via instance relationship graph, in: Proceedings of IEEE Conference on Computer Vision and Pattern Recognition, 2019.

[30] Y. Gong, L. Liu, M. Yang, L.D. Bourdev, Compressing deep convolutional networks using vector quantization, arXiv:1412.6115 [abs].

[31] J. Wu, C. Leng, Y. Wang, Q. Hu, J. Cheng, Quantized convolutional neural networks for mobile devices, in: Proceedings of IEEE Conference on Computer Vision and Pattern Recognition, 2016.

[32] M. Zhu, S. Gupta, To prune, or not to prune: exploring the efficacy of pruning for model compression, arXiv:1710.01878 [abs].

[33] H. Hu, R. Peng, Y.-W. Tai, C.-K. Tang, Network trimming: A data-driven neuron pruning approach towards efficient deep architectures, arXiv:1607.03250 [abs].

[34] P. Molchanov, S. Tyree, T. Karras, T. Aila, J. Kautz, Pruning convolutional neural networks for resource efficient inference, arXiv:1611.06440 [abs].

[35] T. Matiisen, A. Oliver, T. Cohen, J. Schulman, Teacher–student curriculum learning, IEEE Transactions on Neural Networks and Learning Systems 31 (2020) 3732–3740.

[36] J. Gou, B. Yu, S. Maybank, D. Tao, Knowledge distillation: A survey, arXiv:2006.05525 [abs].

[37] Y. Zhang, T. Xiang, T.M. Hospedales, H. Lu, Deep mutual learning, in: Proceedings of IEEE Conference on Computer Vision and Pattern Recognition, 2018.

[38] T. Furlanello, Z.C. Lipton, M. Tschannen, L. Itti, A. Anandkumar, Born again neural networks, in: Proceedings of International Conference on Machine Learning, 2018.

[39] R. Tang, Y. Lu, L. Liu, L. Mou, O. Vechtomova, J.J. Lin, Distilling task-specific knowl-edge from bert into simple neural networks, arXiv:1903.12136 [abs].

[40] S. Zagoruyko, N. Komodakis, Paying more attention to attention: Improving the per-formance of convolutional neural networks via attention transfer, arXiv:1612.03928 [abs].

[41] J. Yim, D. Joo, J.-H. Bae, J. Kim, A gift from knowledge distillation: Fast optimization, network minimization and transfer learning, in: Proceedings of IEEE Conference on Computer Vision and Pattern Recognition, 2017.

[42] G. Chen, W. Choi, X. Yu, T. Han, M. Chandraker, Learning efficient object detection models with knowledge distillation, in: Proceedings of International Conference on Neural Information Processing Systems, 2017.

CHAPTER 4

Mix-precision model encoding and quantization

4.1 Background and challenges

This chapter is based on our related publication [1]. Research on mix-precision activation compression for efficient neural computing is an emerging popular topic, which reveals great potential for a variety of edge-computing and computer vision applications [2–5]. Both stochastic and deterministic approaches were proposed for neural network activation quantization [6–9], which adopted various quantization functions to reduce the precision of activation representation while training the neural network. Though the loss of activation precision causes notable loss of classification accuracy, by reducing the number of bits required the deep neural networks with quantized activation could improve both memory and time efficiency by orders of magnitude compared with the standard floating-point implementation [7,10–12].

One challenge of the researches on activation quantization is the lack of theoretical ground [13]. The performance of existing approaches relies on their choices of quantization strategy, and no minimal loss of representation precision can be determined given the average code rate. Recently, the concept of information theory has attracted attention for its potential for bringing a better understanding of the deep learning optimization process [14,15]. The key idea of these approaches is maintaining the most valuable information of a signal $\mathbf{X}$ using a short code $\hat{\mathbf{X}}$. In the context of deep neural network, $\hat{\mathbf{X}}$ is the signal of quantized activation, and we formalize this problem as that of finding a short code $\hat{\mathbf{X}}$ that preserves the maximum information about $\mathbf{X}$, that is, how to minimize the loss of the information caused by signal quantization through a "bottleneck" in the deep neural network.

Emerging research on neural encoding based on the information theory is an interesting topic, which attempts to answer the basic questions about the design principle of deep networks such as the optimal architecture and the optimal quantization scheme. Recently proposed deep neural networks with information bottlenecks usually have an encoder–decoder architecture for *featurewise* compression, which treat the neural network as a trade-off between compression and prediction [14,16]. As far as we know, this work is the first attempt at bitwise compression addressing the challenge of minimizing the code rate while optimally preserving activation integrity.

Despite information theory has motivated researches, the research on deterministic or stochastic model-based activation quantization is also attracting more attention lately. Lee et al. [17] quantized neural networks according to the channel-level distribution. Zhao et al. [18] used outlier channel splitting to eliminate the effect of outliers caused by quantization. Minimum mean squared error [19] and complementary approach [20] were both used for reducing quantization error. Meanwhile, the research on data–driven activation quantization was also booming. Qiu et al. [21] presented a Fisher vector method to encode activation with a fixed-point number using a deep generative model. Jacob et al. [22] quantized both the activations and weights as 8-bit integers using an iterative approach. Li et al. [23] proposed an entropy-based method for interpretable quantization. Compared with information theory-based methods, these approaches were generally based on different assumptions on the quantization function, and many researchers used nonderivative quantization operation [21–23], which may lead to uninterpretable and suboptimal results.

Technically, in this chapter, we introduce the Bitwise Bottleneck approach, which is based on the *rate-distortion theory* [24]. As a lossy data compression operation, the Bitwise Bottleneck method attempts to determine the most significant bits in the activation by minimizing the quantization distortion. To achieve this, the Bitwise Bottleneck approach directly minimizes the distortion of quantization given the constraint of the maximum code rate of the compressed activation. Specifically, the bitwise bottleneck optimization is formulated as a sparse convex optimization problem, which attempts to minimize the distortion given the constrained code rate. Since the nonsignificant bits generally have near-zero coefficients, the activation can be optimally compressed in a bitwise way.

The contributions of this chapter are threefold. First, it presents an information theory-based method, Bitwise Bottleneck, for *bitwise activation quantization* and compression, which is the first attempt to optimize *bitwise bottleneck* for DNN activation quantization. Second, the code rates of different bottlenecks can be tuned adaptably by a single hyperparameter of the threshold of peak-signal-to-noise ratio (PSNR) loss, allowing the proposed method to flexibly make a trade-off between efficiency and accuracy for different applications. Finally, the bitwise bottleneck minimizes the loss of information caused by activation quantization; therefore, the proposed method suffers almost no loss of classification accuracy while obtaining more than six times improved memory and computational efficiency.

4.2 Rate-distortion theory and sparse encoding

Recently, there has been growing interest in applying information theory to deep neural network activation compression. By interpreting the deep neural network as a lossy data compression approach, the black box of the deep neural network may be opened, and its performance can be optimized by the tool of the rate–distortion theory, which is widely applied in the area of telecommunications [15].

4.2.1 Rate-distortion theory

Let the random variable $\mathbf{X}^{(l)} \in \mathbb{R}^{P \times Q \times K}$ be the floating-point neural network activation tensor associated with the lth layer, where P, Q, K are respectively the height, width, and number of feature maps at the lth layer. The common quantization function $\mathcal{Q}$ can be written as

$$\hat{\mathbf{X}}^{(l)} = \mathcal{Q}(\mathbf{X}^{(l)}), \tag{4.1}$$

where $\hat{\mathbf{X}}^{(l)}$ is the fixed-point representation of the floating-point activation. The goal of lossy data compression is to achieve minimal distortion given the constraint of the maximum code rate. Let g be the function that indicates the number of bits of the given data. According to the rate-distortion theory, the typical lossy data compression approach attempts to minimize the distortion function d given the maximum number of bits η as

$$\min_{\mathcal{Q}(\cdot)} \mathbb{E}(d(\mathbf{X}^{(l)}, \mathcal{Q}(\mathbf{X}^{(l)}))) \quad \text{s.t.} \ \mathbb{E}(g(\hat{\mathbf{X}}^{(l)})) \leq \eta. \tag{4.2}$$

In practice, the quantization function $\mathcal{Q}$ is nondifferentiable and nonconvex due to its integer output, which makes Eq. (4.2) difficult to solve. Different from typical rounding-based quantization approaches that settle for suboptimal solutions, this chapter attempts to find the optimal solution by reformulating Eq. (4.2) as a sparse coding problem.

4.2.2 Activation quantization via bitwise bottleneck encoding

In practice, we could approximate the solution of Eq. (4.2) using a training sample set. Assume $\mathbf{X}_i^{(l)} \in \mathbb{R}^{P \times Q \times K}$ is the floating-point activation tensor

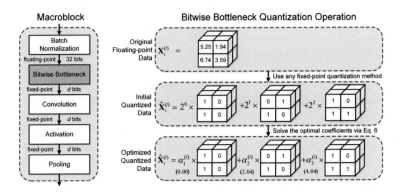

Figure 4.1 Illustration of the Bitwise Bottleneck approach. The bitwise bottleneck operation can be inserted in the convolutional neural network for activation quantization. The idea of the proposed method is to substitute the constant levels of the standard quantization, which are the power of two in this example, for variable coefficients. By exploiting the sparsity of the bitwise coefficients, the bottleneck could reduce the number of bits required for activation representation.

associated with the ith sample output by the lth layer. Fig. 4.1 illustrates the Bitwise Bottleneck approach. Formally speaking, assume $\hat{\mathbf{X}}_i^{(l)}$ is the D-bit fixed-point approximation of $\mathbf{X}_i^{(l)}$ as defined in Eq. (4.3), where $\hat{\mathbf{X}}_{ij}^{(l)} \in \{0, 1\}^{P \times Q \times K}$ is a three-dimensional binary tensor representing the jth bit of $\hat{\mathbf{X}}_i^{(l)}$.

$$\hat{\mathbf{X}}_i^{(l)} = \mathcal{Q}(\mathbf{X}_i^{(l)}) = 2^0 \hat{\mathbf{X}}_{i1}^{(l)} + 2^1 \hat{\mathbf{X}}_{i2}^{(l)} + \ldots + 2^{D-1} \hat{\mathbf{X}}_{iD}^{(l)} \qquad (4.3)$$

where each bitwise data matrix is assigned a constant coefficient of $2^0, \ldots, 2^{D-1}$. In practice, this bitwise activation representation allows the computation of fixed-point data to be implemented in a bitwise way. The computational and memory complexity is proportional to the number of bits of different representations.

Technically, the binary quantization of Eq. (4.3) inherently assumes that each of the D bits in the activation representation is needed, although different bits contain different but *fixed* amounts of information. By removing this assumption the proposed method substitutes the fixed coefficient for a variable $\boldsymbol{\alpha}^{(l)} \in \mathbb{R}^D$ as

$$\hat{\mathbf{X}}_i^{(l)} = \mathcal{Q}(\mathbf{X}_i^{(l)}) = \alpha_1^{(l)} \hat{\mathbf{X}}_{i1}^{(l)} + \alpha_2^{(l)} \hat{\mathbf{X}}_{i2}^{(l)} + \cdots + \alpha_D^{(l)} \hat{\mathbf{X}}_{iD}^{(l)}. \qquad (4.4)$$

The Bitwise Bottleneck approach treats the design of neural networks as a trade-off between compression and prediction, which assumes that the

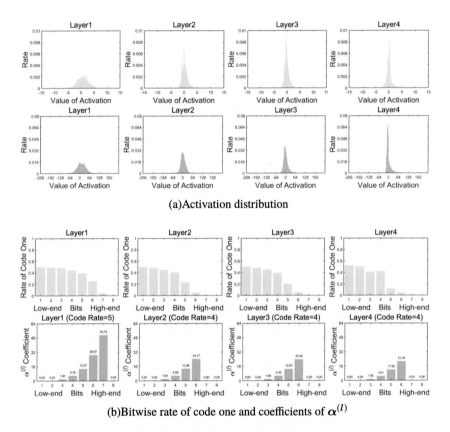

(a)Activation distribution

(b)Bitwise rate of code one and coefficients of $\alpha^{(l)}$

Figure 4.2 Featurewise vs. bitwise activation sparsity. (a) The distributions of real-valued (upper) and quantized (lower) activations of the first four layers of ResNet50 over CIFAR10. (b) The average rate of code one of each bit of the quantized activation (upper) and the estimated coefficients $\alpha^{(l)}$ (lower). It seems that the optimal code rates of different layers depend on the level of activation sparsity, and the Bitwise Bottleneck approach can adaptively remove the near-zero high-end bits and the less-informative low-end bits of the activation representation.

bitwise bottlenecks can exploit the sparsity in the activation representation so that the precision of activation representation without hurting classification accuracy can be reduced. Fig. 4.2 illustrates the activation distributions of the first four layers of ResNet50 [25] over the CIFAR10 dataset. It seems that activations of different layers are sparse, but the sparsity varies from layer to layer. Fig. 4.2(b) illustrates the average rate of code one in each bit of the activation representation (upper graph). Despite the change of featurewise sparsity as shown in Fig. 4.2(a), the bitwise sparsity over the high-end bits of activation representation is easier to detect. Therefore we might be able to estimate the optimal and sparse coefficients $\boldsymbol{\alpha}^{(l)}$ associated with the most significant bits.

According to the rate-distortion theory (Eq. (4.2)), the Bitwise Bottleneck attempts to find the optimal quantization scheme by minimizing the standard squared distortion rate over N training samples given that less than η bitwise coefficients are nonzero,

$$\underset{\boldsymbol{\alpha}^{(l)}}{\arg\min} \sum_{i=1}^{N} \| \mathbf{X}_i^{(l)} - \sum_{j=1}^{D} \alpha_j^{(l)} \hat{\mathbf{X}}_{ij}^{(l)} \|_2^2 \quad \text{s.t. } \|\boldsymbol{\alpha}^{(l)}\|_0 \le \eta, \tag{4.5}$$

where $\hat{\mathbf{X}}_{ij}^{(l)}$ calculated by initial quantization operation is usually known as the quantization *codebook*. In practice, different initial quantization operations can be applied, and Eq. (4.3) is a simple example of the rounding quantization approach. It is worth noting that since the number of nonzero coefficients in $\boldsymbol{\alpha}^{(l)}$ equals the number of bits in the fixed-point representation, the constraint function of Eq. (4.5) actually limits the maximum number of bits in the quantized representation as required by the rate-distortion theory. Recent research shows that Eq. (4.5) is equivalent to the following L1-norm-based problem when fulfilling the sparsity requirement, which leads to a sparse solution [26]:

$$\underset{\boldsymbol{\alpha}^{(l)}}{\arg\min} \sum_{i=1}^{N} \| \mathbf{X}_i^{(l)} - \sum_{j=1}^{D} \alpha_j^{(l)} \hat{\mathbf{X}}_{ij}^{(l)} \|_2^2 \quad \text{s.t. } \|\boldsymbol{\alpha}^{(l)}\|_1 \le \eta. \tag{4.6}$$

The bitwise bottleneck operation solves Eq. (4.6) to determine the sparse significant bits and leads to the minimal distortion. In practice, Eq. (4.6) is usually calculated by solving its Lagrangian form as

$$\underset{\boldsymbol{\alpha}^{(l)}}{\arg\min} \sum_{i=1}^{N} \| \mathbf{X}_i^{(l)} - \sum_{j=1}^{D} \alpha_j^{(l)} \hat{\mathbf{X}}_{ij}^{(l)} \|_2^2 + \lambda \|\boldsymbol{\alpha}^{(l)}\|_1, \tag{4.7}$$

where λ is the hyperparameter for controlling the trade-off between the optimized error rate and the code rate. Eq. (4.6) generally leads to a sparse solution of the coefficients $\boldsymbol{\alpha}^{(l)}$, so the activation bits associated with zero coefficients are removed during the inference stage. To avoid expensive computations caused by floating-point, we quantize the coefficient vector $\boldsymbol{\alpha}^{(l)}$ during the retraining process; therefore, the computational efficiency can be significantly improved.

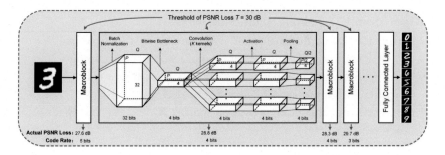

Figure 4.3 Deep neural network with bitwise bottleneck layers. The second macroblock is extended and shown in detail. By setting a single hyperparameter of the threshold of PSNR loss the bitwise bottlenecks in different macroblocks can be trained to flexibly quantize the normalized activations with different optimal code rates.

4.3 Bitwise bottleneck quantization methods

In this section, we introduce the neural network with bitwise bottleneck and the training algorithm for the sparse bitwise bottleneck.

4.3.1 Neural network with bitwise bottlenecks

As shown in Eq. (4.6), the bitwise bottleneck operation calculates the optimal coefficients associated with different bits of the compressed activation representation so that a minimal distortion can be achieved given the maximum code rate. This section shows how the bitwise bottlenecks work in the deep neural network.

Fig. 4.3 shows an example of efficient neural computing with bitwise bottlenecks. The whole network is built based on the classic ResNet, although the bitwise bottleneck operation can be easily integrated into different networks. In practice the bitwise bottleneck operation can be inserted in the macroblock of the deep neural network. A typical macroblock contains a bitwise bottleneck layer, a convolution layer, a pooling layer (optional), a batch normalization layer, and an activation layer. Thanks to the bitwise bottleneck layer, which transforms the normalized floating-point activation to compressed fixed-point activation, the convolution layer can substitute the efficient fixed-point bitwise multiplications for the computationally expensive floating-point multiplications.

The benefits of inserting the bitwise bottlenecks in deep neural networks are twofold. From the perspective of *memory efficiency*, compared with the standard deep neural networks using 32-bit single-precision activation representation, the bitwise bottlenecks can compress the activation

---

Algorithm 4.1: Training Algorithm.

Input: Pretrained floating-point CNN model Θ, threshold of PSNR loss T, number of layers L, number of training samples N, number of bits for initial quantization D;

Output: An Optimized Quantized model $\hat{\Theta}$;

1 Obtain the floating-point activation tensors $\mathbf{X}_i^{(1)}, ..., \mathbf{X}_i^{(L)}$ of Θ for each sample;

2 **for** $l = 1, ..., L$ **do**

3   **while** $t^{(l)} < T$ **do**

4   **for** $i = 1, ..., N$ **do**

5   Obtain the codebook $\hat{\mathbf{X}}_{i1}^{(l)}, \hat{\mathbf{X}}_{i2}^{(l)}, ..., \hat{\mathbf{X}}_{iD}^{(l)}$ by initial quantization of $\mathbf{X}_i^{(l)}$;

6   Obtain the coefficient vector $\boldsymbol{\alpha}^{(l)}$ via Eq. (4.6) and restore $\hat{\mathbf{X}}_i^{(l)}$ via Eq. (4.4);

7   Compute the PSNR loss between $\hat{\mathbf{X}}_i^{(l)}$ and $\mathbf{X}_i^{(l)}$ as $t_i^{(l)}$;

8   **end**

9        $t^{(l)} = \max(t_i^{(l)})$ for each $i = 1, ..., N$;

10   Increase λ;

11   **end**

12 **end**

13 Insert the bottleneck layers into Θ as a new model $\hat{\Theta}$;

14 Refine and quantize the weights and the vector $\boldsymbol{\alpha}^{(l)}$ of $\hat{\Theta}$ by backpropagation until reaching convergence.

---

into arbitrary low-precision (1 to 8 bits), obtaining an improvement in memory efficiency by 32 to 4 times. From the perspective of *computational efficiency*, single-precision floating-point multiplication generally requires considerably more hardware resources and calculation time compared with fixed-point multiplication. By employing the bitwise bottleneck layers before the convolution layers (as shown in Fig. 4.1) the inference latency of deep neural networks may be reduced by over 90%, as indicated in early research [27].

4.3.2 Training sparse bitwise bottlenecks

In practice the sparsity level of the activation may vary from layer to layer in the neural network. It is desired that different macroblocks should use different quantization precisions. As one of the advantages of the proposed method, the optimal code rates of different bitwise bottlenecks can be approximated by tuning a single hyperparameter, which is the threshold of peak-signal-to-noise ratio (PSNR) loss. The measurement of the PSNR is defined as $PSNR = 10 \log_{10} \left(\frac{(2^D-1)^2}{MSE} \right)$, where $MSE = \frac{1}{P \times Q \times K} \| \mathbf{X}_i^{(l)} - \sum_{j=1}^{D} \alpha_j^{(l)} \hat{\mathbf{X}}_{ij}^{(l)} \|_2^2$. By increasing the hyperparameter of λ and comparing the PSNR loss with the threshold each layer can independently approximate the respective acceptable minimal code rate. More detailed information about the training algorithm can be found in Algorithm 4.1.

An illustrative example of training the neural network with multiple bitwise bottlenecks is shown in Fig. 4.2. A closer look at the image reveals three interesting observations. First, the statistical phenomenon of bitwise sparsity exists. Specifically, the high-end bits of the activation representation are statistically near-zero for different layers of the neural network, which validates our assumption. Second, the optimal code rates of different layers depend on the level of activation sparsity. As an example, the activations of the first macroblock of ResNet50 are less sparse than those of the next three macroblocks, resulting in a higher acceptable minimal code rate. Third, it seems that the bitwise bottlenecks can *adaptively* reduce the coefficients $\alpha_j^{(l)}$ of both near-zero high-end bits and less-informative low-end bits of the activation representation.

4.4 Application to efficient image classification

In this section, we demonstrate the effectiveness of the proposed method for efficient image classification through some experiments.

4.4.1 Experiment setting

The experiments were performed on three standard benchmarks: the MNIST [28], CIFAR10 [29], and ImageNet (ILSVRC2012) [30] datasets. The MNIST dataset of 28×28 monochrome images contained 60 thousand training samples and 10 thousand test samples. The CIFAR10 dataset of 32×32 color images contained 50 thousand training samples and 10 thousand test samples, which had 10 classes. The ImageNet dataset contained 1.28 million training samples, 50 thousand verification samples, 100 thousand test samples, and 1000 classes.

The proposed Bitwise Bottleneck approach required an initial quantization operation to calculate the binary activation codebook at the first

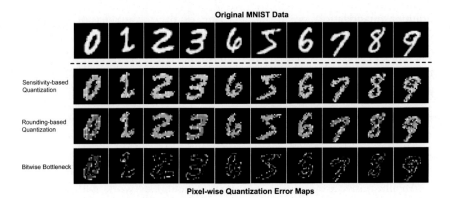

Figure 4.4 The bitwise bottleneck layer can compress the images using 5-bit representation, which is compared with the standard rounding-based quantization and sensitivity-based quantization methods. The error maps of pixelwise absolute values of the difference between the compressed images and the original images are shown.

step. Two different initial quantization methods were adopted, including the Iterative Rounding method [31] and the DoReFa-Net method [8]. The Iterative Rounding method quantized the activation during the iterative backpropagation training process, which was widely used for deep neural network quantization. To validate our method, the standard average classification accuracy over the test dataset was used as the evaluation criterion. The results of the proposed method were achieved based on the ResNet50, and all the compared approaches were also based on ResNet50 for fair comparison.

All the experiments were performed on a computer equipped with Intel i7-7800X CPU and 2 NVIDIA TITAN Xp GPU. Similarly to other studies, a backpropagation-based training process was adopted in the proposed method to refine and quantize the weight parameters of the deep neural network and the coefficients $\alpha^{(l)}$. In experiments the ADAM [32] algorithm was applied to implement the backpropagation process, where the learning rate was 0.0001, and the batch size was 64. We retrained 4000 iterations on the MNIST and CIFAR10 datasets and 5 epochs on the ImageNet dataset.

4.4.2 Visualization and analysis

A group of experiments were performed over the MNIST dataset to analyze and visualize the performance of the proposed method compared with the initial and other quantization approaches. The bitwise bottlenecks reduced the code rate of the fixed-point representation from the initial quantization length of D bits to the effective code rate d, which was the number of nonzero coefficients in vector $\boldsymbol{\alpha}^{(l)}$ (Eq. (4.6)). Fig. 4.4 visualized the loss of activation integrity caused by 5-bit activation quantization over the MNIST dataset. The absolute values of the difference between the compressed image data and the original image data were compared between the proposed method and the baseline quantization methods. In summary, the proposed Bitwise Bottleneck method showed the highest PSNR (47.30 ± 0.51 dB) for activation quantization compared with the standard rounding-based method (42.02 ± 0.54 dB) and sensitivity-based method (34.94 ± 0.84 dB) [33].

Fig. 4.5(a) shows the relation between the effective code rate d and the average PSNR achieved over the MNIST dataset. Overall, the proposed Bitwise Bottleneck approach achieved 1.98 dB to 12.44 dB higher PSNR compared with the classic rounding-based quantization and sensitivity-based quantization methods. The superiority of PSNR was consistent when different numbers of nonzero coefficients were chosen, which can be controlled by the hyperparameter of λ, as shown in the figure.

Similarly to other activation quantization approaches, a backpropagation retraining process was applied after the activation quantization process to refine the weight parameters and the coefficients $\boldsymbol{\alpha}^{(l)}$ that were quantized to D bits with a rounding-based approach. Fig. 4.5(b) shows the final classification accuracy achieved with backpropagation. The average accuracy over both the MNIST and CIFAR10 datasets was evaluated with various numbers of nonzero coefficients d. Experimental results showed that the proposed method outperformed the baseline approach when fewer than four bits were used for activation quantization. The loss of accuracy caused by the rounding-based quantization became worse when the dataset was more complicated, whereas the Bitwise Bottleneck approach suffered almost no loss of accuracy compared with the floating-point model when more than three bits were used for activation representation.

The Bitwise Bottleneck approach featured its ability to automatically determine the effective code rates of different layers. By setting the threshold of PSNR loss accepted for activation quantization, the bitwise bottlenecks can estimate the minimal effective code rate by the sparse optimization. Fig. 4.5(c) shows the relation among the threshold of PSNR loss, the average effective code rate across different layers, and the classification accuracy. As shown in experiments over the CIFAR10 dataset, the classification accuracy decreased when the threshold of PSNR loss increased. However,

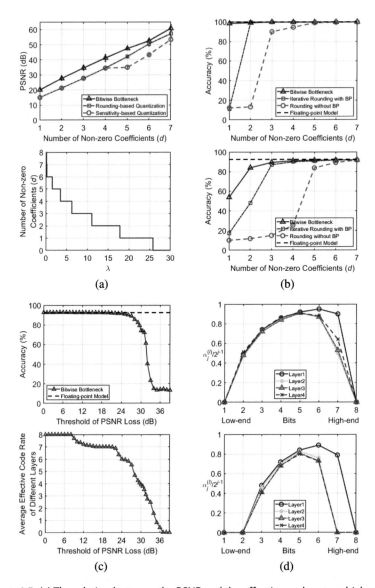

Figure 4.5 (a) The relation between the PSNR and the effective code rate, which equals the number of nonzero coefficients in $\alpha^{(l)}$, and the relation between the effective code rate and the value of λ. (b) Accuracy of the deep neural network with bitwise bottlenecks over the MNIST (upper) and CIFAR10 (lower) datasets, which can compress the activation of the deep neural network with different effective code rates d. (c) The change in accuracy and average effective code rate of different layers when using the bitwise bottlenecks to compress the 8-bit fixed-point activation according to different PSNR loss thresholds. (d) The ratio of $\alpha_j^{(l)}/2^{j-1}$ with different thresholds of PSNR loss ($T = 26$ upper, $T = 30$ lower).

when the PSNR loss was less than 24 dB, almost no decrease in classification accuracy was detected (less than 1%). The accuracy began to decrease when fewer than 6 bits on average were used for activation representation.

The Bitwise Bottlenecks approach handled the task of activation quantization as a trade-off between compression and prediction. Fig. 4.5(d) shows the ratio of $\alpha_j^{(l)}/2^{j-1}$ for each bit of the quantized activation, where 2^{j-1} is the natural coefficient of Eq. (4.3), which reflects how much information the jth bit contains. Two interesting observations can be found in the image. First, the low-end bits of the activation representation were removed by the bottlenecks, leading to minimal loss of information caused by bitwise compression. Second, despite containing more information, the high-end bits were also removed by the bottlenecks, which was caused by the bitwise sparsity in high-end bits (as shown in Fig. 4.2).

4.4.3 Comparison with the state-of-the-art approaches

The proposed method was evaluated with the state-of-the-art activation quantization approaches over the ImageNet dataset. The original floating-point model and the proposed Bitwise Bottleneck approach were compared with the DSQ [34], ACIQ [20], Focused Compression [35], Integer-only [22], UNIQ [36], INQ [37], DoReFa-Net [8], and Iterative Rounding [31] approaches. Thresholds of PSNR loss of 8 dB and 16 dB were adopted to quantize the activations, which resulted in an average effective code rate of 5.0 ($\pm$1) and 4.0 ($\pm$1) bits. The quantization method of DoReFa-Net [8] was adopted for initial quantization. The standard TensorFlow quantization tool was used to quantize the weights to 8 bits, and all the coefficients of $\alpha^{(l)}$ were quantized to 6 bits.

We found in our experiments that most quantization methods could achieve almost the same accuracy as the floating-point model with 6- to 8-bits activation representation, but at 5-bit and below the accuracy began to drop obviously. Table 4.1 summarizes the results of classification accuracy over the ImageNet dataset. As shown in the table, the top-1 accuracy loss of 5-bit activation representation was up to 3.5%, and top-1 accuracy loss of 4-bit activation representation was between 1.8% and 5.6%. However, the Bitwise Bottleneck method could achieve marginal loss of accuracy at 5-bit and 4-bit. The loss of accuracy at 4-bit was 0.8%, which was 4.7% higher than that of the initial quantization method (DoReFa-Net). Moreover, the Bitwise Bottleneck method exceeded the Integer-only method with 8-bit activation and the INQ and Focused Compression methods with 32-bit floating-point activation.

Table 4.1 Comparison with state-of-the-art approaches over the ImageNet dataset.

Method	Year	Weights	Activations	Top-1 Acc (%)	Top-5 Acc (%)
Floating-point Model	2016	32	32	75.6	92.8
Bitwise Bottleneck	–	8	5	**75.7**	**92.7**
DSQ	2019	8	5	75.2	92.5
Focused Compression	2019	5	32	74.9	92.6
Integer-only	2018	8	8	74.9	–
INQ	2017	5	32	74.8	92.5
DoReFa-Net (initial quantization)	2016	8	5	73.8	91.7
Iterative Rounding	2014	8	5	72.1	90.4
Bitwise Bottleneck	–	8	4	**74.8**	**92.2**
DSQ	2019	8	4	73.8	91.7
UNIQ	2018	4	8	73.4	–
ACIQ	2019	8	4	71.8	–
DoReFa-Net (initial quantization)	2016	8	4	70.1	89.3
Iterative Rounding	2014	8	4	70.0	89.4

4.4.4 Efficiency improvement

From the perspective of reducing computational complexity, when the neural network was implemented in a bitwise way, a lower code rate led to linearly fewer bitwise operations. Taking the 8-bit fixed-point representation as an example, each fixed-point operation could be implemented by 8 bitwise operations, and if we cut off 1 bit, then the number of operations could be reduced by 12.5%. In addition, by reducing a single bit the hardware source requirement was also reduced by 12.5% when it was implemented using dedicated hardware. Generally, compared with the 32-bit activations representation, the bitwise bottlenecks could improve the computational efficiency by more than 6.4 times without hurting the performance of the deep neural network. Besides, considering the weights were quantized to 8-bit, the computational efficiency improvement could reach 25.6 times.

From the perspective of reducing memory occupation, reducing the activation code rate linearly reduced the memory requirement. The activation of a standard neural network was usually represented by 32-bit floating-point, which occupied 4 bytes of memory. However, the bitwise bottlenecks could compress them to fewer than 5 bits without hurting the classification accuracy, where the running memory could be reduced by 84%.

References

[1] X. Zhou, K. Liu, C. Shi, H. Liu, J. Liu, Optimizing information theory based bitwise bottlenecks for efficient mixed-precision activation quantization, in: Proceedings of AAAI Conference on Artificial Intelligence, vol. 35, 2021, pp. 3590–3598.

[2] C. Chen, A. Seff, A. Kornhauser, J. Xiao, DeepDriving: Learning affordance for direct perception in autonomous driving, in: Proceedings of IEEE International Conference on Computer Vision, 2015, pp. 2722–2730.

[3] B. Wu, F. Iandola, P.H. Jin, K. Keutzer, SqueezeDet: Unified, small, low power fully convolutional neural networks for real-time object detection for autonomous driving, in: Proceedings of IEEE Conference on Computer Vision and Pattern Recognition, 2017, pp. 129–137.

[4] C. McCool, T. Perez, B. Upcroft, Mixtures of lightweight deep convolutional neural networks: Applied to agricultural robotics, IEEE Robotics and Automation Letters 2 (3) (2017) 1344–1351.

[5] H. Xu, Y. Gao, F. Yu, T. Darrell, End-to-end learning of driving models from large-scale video datasets, in: Proceedings of IEEE Conference on Computer Vision and Pattern Recognition, 2017, pp. 2174–2182.

[6] S. Gupta, A. Agrawal, K. Gopalakrishnan, P. Narayanan, Deep learning with limited numerical precision, in: Proceedings of International Conference on Machine Learning, 2015, pp. 1737–1746.

[7] M. Courbariaux, Y. Bengio, J.P. David, BinaryConnect: Training deep neural networks with binary weights during propagations, in: Proceedings of International Conference on Neural Information Processing Systems, 2015, pp. 3123–3131.

[8] S. Zhou, Y. Wu, Z. Ni, X. Zhou, H. Wen, Y. Zou, DoReFa-Net: Training low bitwidth convolutional neural networks with low bitwidth gradients, arXiv:1606.06160 [abs].

[9] J. Wu, C. Leng, Y. Wang, Q. Hu, J. Cheng, Quantized convolutional neural networks for mobile devices, in: Proceedings of the IEEE Conference on Computer Vision and Pattern Recognition, 2016, pp. 4820–4828.

[10] M. Kim, P. Smaragdis, Bitwise neural networks, arXiv:1601.06071 [abs].

[11] M. Courbariaux, I. Hubara, D. Soudry, R. El-Yaniv, Y. Bengio, Binarized neural networks: Training deep neural networks with weights and activations constrained to +1 or −1, arXiv:1602.02830 [abs].

[12] M. Rastegari, V. Ordonez, J. Redmon, A. Farhadi, XNOR-Net: ImageNet classification using binary convolutional neural networks, in: Proceedings of European Conference on Computer Vision, 2016, pp. 525–542.

[13] V. Sze, Y.-H. Chen, T.-J. Yang, J.S. Emer, Efficient processing of deep neural networks: A tutorial and survey, Proceedings of the IEEE 105 (12) (2017) 2295–2329.

[14] N. Tishby, N. Zaslavsky, Deep learning and the information bottleneck principle, in: Proceedings of IEEE Information Theory Workshop, 2015, pp. 1–5.

[15] R. Shwartz-Ziv, N. Tishby, Opening the black box of deep neural networks via information, arXiv:1703.00810 [abs].

[16] B. Dai, C. Zhu, D. Wipf, Compressing neural networks using the variational information bottleneck, arXiv:1802.10399 [abs].

[17] J.H. Lee, S. Ha, S. Choi, W.-J. Lee, S. Lee, Quantization for rapid deployment of deep neural networks, arXiv:1810.05488 [abs].

[18] R. Zhao, Y. Hu, J. Dotzel, C. De Sa, Z. Zhang, Improving neural network quantization using outlier channel splitting, arXiv preprint, arXiv:1901.09504, 2019.

[19] E. Kravchik, F. Yang, P. Kisilev, Y. Choukroun, Low-bit quantization of neural networks for efficient inference, in: Proceedings of IEEE International Conference on Computer Vision, 2019.

[20] R. Banner, Y. Nahshan, D. Soudry, Post training 4-bit quantization of convolutional networks for rapid-deployment, in: Proceedings of International Conference on Neural Information Processing Systems, 2019, pp. 7948–7956.

[21] Z. Qiu, T. Yao, T. Mei, Deep quantization: Encoding convolutional activations with deep generative model, in: Proceedings of IEEE Conference on Computer Vision and Pattern Recognition, 2017, pp. 6759–6768.

[22] B. Jacob, S. Kligys, B. Chen, M. Zhu, M. Tang, A. Howard, H. Adam, D. Kalenichenko, Quantization and training of neural networks for efficient integer-arithmetic-only inference, in: Proceedings of IEEE Conference on Computer Vision and Pattern Recognition, 2018, pp. 2704–2713.

[23] Y. Li, S. Lin, B. Zhang, J. Liu, D. Doermann, Y. Wu, F. Huang, R. Ji, Exploiting kernel sparsity and entropy for interpretable CNN compression, in: Proceedings of IEEE Conference on Computer Vision and Pattern Recognition, 2019, pp. 2800–2809.

[24] T. Berger, Rate-Distortion Theory, Wiley Encyclopedia of Telecommunications, 2003, https://doi.org/10.1002/0471219282.eot142.

[25] K. He, X. Zhang, S. Ren, J. Sun, Deep residual learning for image recognition, in: Proceedings of IEEE Conference on Computer Vision and Pattern Recognition, 2016, pp. 770–778.

[26] R.G. Baraniuk, Compressive sensing [lecture notes], IEEE Signal Processing Magazine 24 (4) (2007) 118–121.

[27] X. Zhou, S. Li, F. Tang, S. Hu, Z. Lin, L. Zhang, DANoC: An efficient algorithm and hardware codesign of deep neural networks on chip, IEEE Transactions on Neural Networks and Learning Systems 29 (2018) 3176–3187.

[28] Y. LeCun, L. Bottou, Y. Bengio, P. Haffner, et al., Gradient-based learning applied to document recognition, Proceedings of the IEEE 86 (11) (1998) 2278–2324.

[29] A. Krizhevsky, G. Hinton, et al., Learning multiple layers of features from tiny images, Tech. rep., Citeseer, 2009.

[30] J. Deng, W. Dong, R. Socher, L.-J. Li, K. Li, L. Fei-Fei, ImageNet: A large-scale hierarchical image database, in: Proceedings of IEEE Conference on Computer Vision and Pattern Recognition, 2009, pp. 248–255.

[31] M. Courbariaux, Y. Bengio, J.-P. David, Training deep neural networks with low precision multiplications, arXiv:1412.7024 [abs].

[32] D.P. Kingma, J. Ba, Adam: A method for stochastic optimization, arXiv:1412.6980 [abs].

[33] Y. Li, S. Zhang, X. Zhou, F. Ren, Build a compact binary neural network through bit-level sensitivity and data pruning, Neurocomputing 398 (2020) 45–54.

[34] R. Gong, X. Liu, S. Jiang, T. Li, P. Hu, J. Lin, F. Yu, J. Yan, Differentiable soft quantization: Bridging full-precision and low-bit neural networks, in: Proceedings of IEEE International Conference on Computer Vision, 2019, pp. 4852–4861.

[35] Y. Zhao, X. Gao, D. Bates, R. Mullins, C.-Z. Xu, Focused quantization for sparse CNNs, in: Proceedings of International Conference on Neural Information Processing Systems, 2019, pp. 5585–5594.

[36] C. Baskin, E. Schwartz, E. Zheltonozhskii, N. Liss, R. Giryes, A.M. Bronstein, A. Mendelson, UNIQ: Uniform noise injection for the quantization of neural networks, arXiv:1804.10969 [abs].

[37] A. Zhou, A. Yao, Y. Guo, L. Xu, Y. Chen, Incremental network quantization: Towards lossless CNNs with low-precision weights, arXiv:1702.03044 [abs].

CHAPTER 5

Model encoding of binary neural networks

5.1 Background and challenges

Deep Neural Networks (DNNs) have achieved great success in many different kinds of vision tasks. However, due to the increased computation workload and memory occupation, the deployment of these powerful networks is of great challenge, especially in resource-limited devices.

To address this challenge, many model compression and acceleration methods have been proposed to reduce the memory and computation requirements, such as network pruning [1], weight decomposition [2], lightweight network design [3,4], knowledge distillation [5], and network quantization [6–8]. With the help of these efficient methods, it is possible to deploy powerful DNNs on the embedded devices for different applications such as computer vision and automated driving [9].

As an extreme version of the compressed models, Binary Neural Networks (BNNs) constrain the full-precision weights and activations of DNNs to discrete binary values of $\{-1, +1\}$ [7]. Therefore the memory required by DNN inference is able to be reduced by up to $32\times$ times in theory. By applying BNN methods, energy-hungry operations like floating-point multiplications can be replaced with efficient bitwise operations. However, the BNNs generally suffer a significant loss of classification accuracy. For example, the binary AlexNet using the XNOR-Net method had 12.4% less Top-1 accuracy compared with its full-precision baseline model [10].

One strategy to boost the accuracy was incorporating a larger volume of binary parameters in the BNNs. ABC-Net [11] approximated full-precision counterparts by using the linear combination of multiple binary bases. Following a similar way, Group-Net [12] proposed to combine the multiple homogeneous binary branches to reconstruct the full-precision group. On the other hand, BENN [13] suggested using ensemble methods like bagging on multiple parallel BNNs.

The research on hardware-friendly lightweight neural networks with binary weights and activations is recently attracting more attention. BinaryNet [7] quantized both weights and activations to 1-bit values and started

Deep Learning on Edge Computing Devices
https://doi.org/10.1016/B978-0-32-385783-3.00013-2

75

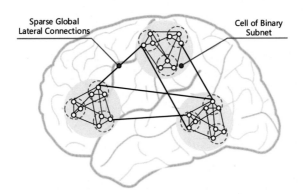

Figure 5.1 Illustration of the brain-inspired Cellular Binary Neural Network (CBN-Net), which consists of multiple cells of binary subnets. Different cells of subnets are connected by learnable sparse global lateral connections.

the research of BNNs. To reduce quantization error, XNOR-Net [10] proposed to introduce channelwise scaling factors, whereas DoReFa-Net [14] used a layerwise scaling factor instead. Bireal-Net [15] proposed to insert fixed shortcuts into BNNs. Circulant BNN [16] proposed a circulant convolution with increased filter diversity which enhanced the representational ability of BNNs. Moreover, ABC-Net [11], BENN [13], and Group-Net [12] all took advantages of multiple binary base modules or models to improve the classification accuracy at the cost of computational efficiency. In summary, the performance of binary neural networks was gradually climbing; however, due to reduced model capacity, there was still a significant performance gap between BNNs and the high-precision deep neural networks [17].

In this chapter, we present another strategy that attempts to explore the optimal network structure of the BNN to improve classification accuracy. As illustrated in Fig. 5.1, the proposed Cellular Binary Neural Network (CBN-Net) features three characteristics inspired by the human brain. Firstly, similarly to the human visual neural network, which consists of multiple subnets [18], the CBN-Net is also a hierarchical network, which consists of multiple *cells of subnets*. Secondly, research showed that different neural subnets were connected by sparse global lateral dendrites in the brain cortex [19]. Likewise, different subnets of the CBN-Net are connected with *sparse* global lateral connections *grouped* with respect to different layers of source neurons. Thirdly, unlike the existing BNNs with

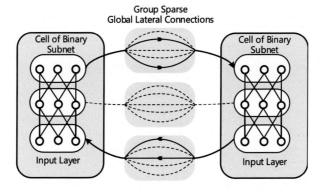

Figure 5.2 A toy example of the proposed CBN-Net, which consists of two cells of feed-forward subnets with binary weights and activations. The channelwise global connections between horizontal layers in different subnets are assumed to be group sparse so that only a small proportion of layers and channels of neurons are laterally connected. The dashed lines indicate removed sparse connections.

fixed network structures, the structure of the lateral connections in CBN-Net is learnable like the human brain [20]. (See Fig. 5.2.)

5.2 The basic of binary neural network

For most binary neural networks, the weights and inputs in convolutional layers were binarized using sign function. We denote the convolutional filters as $\mathbf{W} \in \mathbb{R}^{c_{out} \times c_{in} \times r \times r}$, where c_{out} is the number of filters, c_{in} is the number of input channels, and r is the filter size. The process of weight binarization is $\mathbf{B}_w = \text{sign}(\mathbf{W})$, where $\mathbf{B}_w \in \{+1, -1\}^{c_{out} \times c_{in} \times r \times r}$ denotes the binary weights, $\text{sign}(\cdot)$ generates $+1$ for positive inputs and -1 for negative inputs. To constrain a convolutional neural network to have binary weights, we estimate the real-valued weight filter $\mathbf{W}$ using a binary filter $\mathbf{B}_w$ and a scaling factor $\alpha \in \mathbb{R}$ such that $\mathbf{W} \approx \alpha \mathbf{B}_w$. A convolutional operation ($*$) for $\mathbf{X}$ and $\mathbf{W}$ can be approximated by

$$\mathbf{X} * \mathbf{W} \approx (\mathbf{X} \oplus \mathbf{B}_w)\alpha, \tag{5.1}$$

where $\oplus$ indicates a convolution without any multiplication. Since the weight values are binary, we can implement the convolution with additions and subtractions. The binary weight filters reduce memory usage by a factor of $32\times$ compared to single precision filters. To estimate binary weights $\mathbf{B}_w$, we assume that $\mathbf{W}$ and $\mathbf{B}_w$ are vectors in $\mathbb{R}^n$, where $n = c \times r \times r$. To find an optimal estimation for $\mathbf{W} \approx \alpha \mathbf{B}_w$, we solve the following optimization:

$$\mathcal{L}(\mathbf{B}_w, \alpha) = ||\mathbf{W} - \alpha \mathbf{B}_w||^2,$$
$$\alpha^*, \mathbf{B}_w^* = \arg\min_{\alpha, \mathbf{B}_w} \mathcal{L}(\mathbf{B}_w, \alpha). \qquad (5.2)$$

By expanding Eq. (5.2), we have the following equation:

$$\mathcal{L}(\mathbf{B}_w, \alpha) = \alpha^2 \mathbf{B}_w^T \mathbf{B}_w - 2\alpha \mathbf{W}^T \mathbf{B}_w + \mathbf{W}^T \mathbf{W}. \qquad (5.3)$$

Since $\mathbf{B}_w \in \{+1, -1\}^n$, $\mathbf{B}_w^T \mathbf{B}_w = n$ is a constant, and $\mathbf{W}^T \mathbf{W}$ is also a constant because $\mathbf{W}$ is a known variable. Let us define $c = \mathbf{W}^T \mathbf{W}$. Now we can rewrite Eq. (5.3) as $\mathcal{L}(\mathbf{B}_w, \alpha) = \alpha^2 n - 2\alpha \mathbf{W}^T \mathbf{B}_w + c$. The optimal solution for $\mathbf{B}_w$ can be achieved by maximizing the following constrained optimization (note that α is a positive value in Eq. (5.2), and therefore it can be ignored in the maximization):

$$\mathbf{B}_w^* = \arg\max_{\mathbf{B}_w} \{\mathbf{W}^T \mathbf{B}_w\} \qquad \text{s.t. } \mathbf{B}_w \in \{+1, -1\}^n. \qquad (5.4)$$

This optimization can be solved by assigning $\mathbf{B}_i = +1$ if $W_i \geq 0$ and $\mathbf{B}_i = -1$ if $\mathbf{W}_i < 0$, and therefore the optimal solution is $\mathbf{B}_w^* = \text{sign}(\mathbf{W})$. To find the optimal value for the scaling factor α^*, we take the derivative of $\mathcal{L}$ with respect to α and set it to zero:

$$\alpha^* = \frac{\mathbf{W}^T \mathbf{B}_w^*}{n}. \qquad (5.5)$$

By replacing $\mathbf{B}_w^*$ with $\text{sign}(\mathbf{W})$ we have

$$\alpha^* = \frac{\mathbf{W}^T \text{sign}(\mathbf{W})}{n} = \frac{\sum |\mathbf{W}_i|}{n} = \frac{1}{n}||\mathbf{W}||_{l1}, \qquad (5.6)$$

and therefore the optimal estimation of a binary weight filter can be simply achieved by taking the sign of weight values. The optimal scaling factor is the average of absolute weight values.

The input feature maps of the same convolutional layer are represented by $\mathbf{X} \in \mathbb{R}^{c_{in} \times h \times m}$, where c_{in} is the number of input channels, and h and m are the height and width of feature maps, respectively. We can binarize the input $\mathbf{X}$ in a similar way and get the binary feature maps represented by $\mathbf{B}_x = \text{sign}(\mathbf{X})$. Now we have binary weights and activations, and so the

floating-point computations can be replaced with efficient logical computations, i.e., the XNOR-POPCOUNT operation $\otimes$ [10]:

$$\mathbf{Y} = \alpha(\mathbf{B}_{\mathrm{w}} \otimes \mathbf{B}_{\mathrm{x}}), \tag{5.7}$$

where $\mathbf{Y} \in \mathbb{R}^{c_{\mathrm{out}} \times h \times m}$ is the output of the binary convolutional layer, and α is
the scaling factor. During the training process, we could adopt the widely
used method called Straight Through Estimator (STE) to backpropagate
the gradient through the sign function as follows:

$$\frac{\partial \mathcal{L}}{\partial \mathbf{W}} \approx \mathrm{clip}\left(\frac{\partial \mathcal{L}}{\partial \mathbf{B}_{\mathrm{w}}}, -1, +1\right), \tag{5.8}$$

where clip is a piecewise linear function [21], $\mathcal{L}$ is the total loss function
of the binary neural network, and $\mathbf{W}$ is used as the latent weights to be
optimized during training.

5.3 The cellular binary neural network with lateral connections

In this section, we detailedly introduce the cellular binary neural network
with lateral connections, including cellular binary neural network, group
sparse regularization, loss function, and the training process.

5.3.1 Cellular binary neural network

As shown in Fig. 5.3, the structure of binary neural networks evolves from
using a single pipeline [7] to adopting parallel ensemble pipelines [13] for
more accurate classification. As the third step of evolution, the proposed
CBN-Net attempts to explore the optimal lateral structure connecting different cells of subnets, so as to further improve the classification accuracy
of the binary neural networks.

Formally, the CBN-Net consists of multiple binary subnets, and the
superscript i represents the ith binary subnet, the superscript j represents the jth binary subnet, and superscript k represents the kth binary
layer. For the ith subnet, we denote by $\mathbf{X}^{(i,k)}$ the input of the kth layer
and by $\mathbf{Y}^{(i,k)}$ the output. The lateral connections from the ith subnet
to the jth subnet at the kth layer contain channelwise weights $\overline{W}^{(i,j,k)} =$
$[\overline{W}_1^{(i,j,k)}, \overline{W}_2^{(i,j,k)}, \dots, \overline{W}_{c_{\mathrm{out}}}^{(i,j,k)}]$, where c_{out} is the number of channels.

The CBN-Net takes advantage of brain-inspired global lateral connections, which transmit the features horizontally to different subnets. The tth

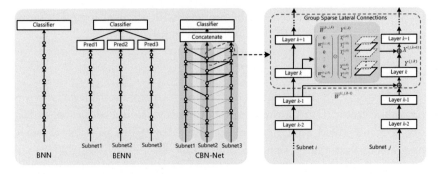

Figure 5.3 The architecture of the Cellular Binary Neural Network. The left subfigure compares the binary neural networks with different architectures. The lateral connection of the CBN-Net contained in the dashed square is magnified on the right. The right subfigure illustrates the channelwise point multiplication operation defined by the group sparse lateral connection. The dashed connections are near-zero sparse connections.

input channel of the jth subnet at the $(k + 1)$th layer $\mathbf{X}_t^{(j,k+1)}$ *may* depend on the tth output channel of the kth layers of different subnets as shown in Fig. 5.3:

$$\mathbf{X}_t^{(j,k+1)} = \mathbf{Y}_t^{(j,k)} + \sum_i^{i \neq j} \overline{W}_t^{(i,j,k)} \mathbf{Y}_t^{(i,k)}, \qquad (5.9)$$

where the *matrix* $\mathbf{Y}_t^{(i,k)}$ is the tth channel of the output tensor $\mathbf{Y}^{(i,k)}$. With the weighted lateral connections, the output features from other binary subnets can enrich the input features of the next layer.

5.3.2 Group sparse regularization

It is worth noting that in Fig. 5.3 the brain–inspired lateral connections are assumed to be *sparse*. Furthermore, since different layers in deep neural networks may play different roles for the task of image classification, the lateral connections of the CBN-Net are assumed to be *grouped* with respect to different source layers. The characteristic of group sparsity can significantly reduce computational complexity caused by the extra lateral connections.

To improve the classification accuracy of the binary neural network, the CBN–Net adopts learnable lateral connection weights $\overline{\mathbf{W}}$ and attempts to explore the optimal routing paths described by the lateral connection weights. Technically, the L21 norm–based group sparse regularization term is adopted:

$$\left\|\overline{\mathbf{W}}\right\|_{2,1} = \sum_{k=1}^{N} \sum_{i,j}^{i \neq j} \|\overline{W}^{(i,j,k)}\|_2, \tag{5.10}$$

where i and j indicate the indices of binary subnets, and N is the total number of binary convolutional layers.

According to Eq. (5.10), all the lateral connection weights associated with the same source layer are treated as a group; therefore by minimizing Eq. (5.10) via regularization the CBN-Net can achieve optimized group sparse lateral connections where both the number of connected layers and the number of channels transmitted can be significantly reduced. Technically, Eq. (5.10) is adopted as a regularization term and incorporated in the loss function. By minimizing the loss function during the training process the redundant lateral connections that have weights of near-zero values can be pruned off, which improves both computation and memory efficiency.

5.3.3 Loss function

One challenge of binarizing full-precision deep neural networks is the shift of output distribution caused by low-precision quantization. To address this challenge, we propose to take advantage of Knowledge Distillation (KD) [5], which uses the full-precision baseline *teacher* model to help to train the *student* binary neural network. More specifically, to optimize the lateral connections of the CBN-Net, the difference of the output distributions between the teacher model and student model is formulated as the following loss function:

$$\mathcal{L}_{KD} = \rho \mathcal{L}_{KL}(\widehat{\mathbf{Y}}^{s_\theta}, \widehat{\mathbf{Y}}^{t_\theta}) + (1 - \rho)\mathcal{L}_{CE}(\widehat{\mathbf{Y}}^{s_\theta}, \mathbf{Y}^g), \tag{5.11}$$

where $\widehat{\mathbf{Y}}^{s_\theta}$ and $\widehat{\mathbf{Y}}^{t_\theta}$ are the soft labels generated by the student model s_θ and teacher model t_θ, respectively, Y^g is the ground truth label, and ρ is the soft ratio, which controls the weight between these two losses. Technically, the Kullback–Leibler (KL) divergence is used in our research to define the first loss of $\mathcal{L}_{KL}$, and the Cross-Entropy (CE) is used to define the second loss of $\mathcal{L}_{CE}$. Before writing the $\mathcal{L}_{KD}$ in detail, we first define the softmax output of a deep neural network as

$$\hat{p}_d = \frac{e^{\hat{y}_d/T}}{\sum_{d=1}^{D} e^{\hat{y}_d/T}}, \tag{5.12}$$

where the temperature T is used to soften the probabilities, d is the class index, and D is the total number of classes. Suppose $\hat{p}_d^{t\theta} \in \mathbb{R}$ and $\hat{p}_d^{s\theta} \in \mathbb{R}$ are the softmax outputs of the teacher and student models at the dth class, respectively, $p_d^{s\theta} \in \mathbb{R}$ is the special case of $\hat{p}_d^{s\theta}$ when $T = 1$. Given an input image, the total loss function of $\mathcal{L}_{\mathrm{KD}}$ can be written as

$$\mathcal{L}_{\mathrm{KD}} = \rho T^2 \sum_{d=1}^{D} (\hat{p}_d^{t\theta} \log \frac{\hat{p}_d^{t\theta}}{\hat{p}_d^{s\theta}}) - (1 - \rho) \sum_{d=1}^{D} y_d^{\mathrm{g}} \log p_d^{s\theta}, \qquad (5.13)$$

where y_d^{g} is the dth element of the vector of ground truth labels. As suggested by [5], we have multiplied the first loss in Eq. (5.13) by T^2 to keep the influence of these two loss functions at the same level during the learning process.

It is worth noting that we only optimize the parameters in the student network, whereas the parameters of the teacher network are fixed during training, so that the term containing the teacher model $\rho T^2 \sum_{d=1}^{D} \hat{p}_d^{t\theta} \log \hat{p}_d^{t\theta}$ in Eq. (5.13) can be omitted in the back-propagation phase. Finally, we derive the knowledge distillation loss function as

$$\mathcal{L}_{\mathrm{KD}} = -\rho T^2 \sum_{d=1}^{D} \hat{p}_d^{t\theta} \log \hat{p}_d^{s\theta} - (1 - \rho) \sum_{d=1}^{D} y_d^{\mathrm{g}} \log p_d^{s\theta}. \qquad (5.14)$$

As Eq. (5.14) demonstrates, the knowledge distillation consists of two cross-entropy losses balanced by a soft ratio ρ. Combining the group sparse regularization term in Eq. (5.10) with knowledge distillation, we derive our final loss function used to train the CBN-Net as follows:

$$\mathcal{L} = \mathcal{L}_{\mathrm{KD}} + \gamma \left\| \overline{\mathbf{W}} \right\|_{2,1}, \qquad (5.15)$$

where γ is a hyperparameter that controls the sparsity of group sparse lateral connections.

5.3.4 Training process

For the backward learning process, a challenge to optimize binary neural networks was reported [17]. As MeliusNet [22] claimed that more gradient flow paths might help the binary models to converge faster, we argue that the paths built by the lateral connections may have a similar ability. In detail, the gradient of the tth output channel through the jth subnet at the kth layer

---

Algorithm 5.1: The Key Steps of Feed-Forward and Back-Propagation Process of the Cellular Binary Neural Network.

---

1 **Require:** Teacher model t_θ, Loss function $\mathcal{L}$, soft ratio ρ, regularization coefficient γ, temperature T, learning rate η.

  1: **Forward Propagation:**
  2: For each subnet j and layer k, obtain the output: $\mathbf{Y}^{(j,k)}$ (Eq. (5.7)) and compute the input of next layer: $\mathbf{X}^{(j,k+1)}$ (Eq. (5.9));
  3: Compute the loss function with the knowledge distillation and regularization term: $\mathcal{L} = \mathcal{L}_{\mathrm{KD}} + \gamma \left\| \overline{\mathbf{W}} \right\|_{2,1}$ (Eq. (5.15)).
  4: **Backward Propagation:**
  5: For each subnet j and layer k, compute the gradient of $\mathbf{W}^{(j,k)}$: $\frac{\partial \mathcal{L}}{\partial \mathbf{W}^{(j,k)}}$ (Eqs. (5.8) and (5.17));
  6: For each subnet pair i, j and layer k, compute the gradients of $\overline{W}^{(i,j,k)}$: $\frac{\partial \mathcal{L}}{\partial \overline{W}^{(i,j,k)}}$ (Eq. (5.18)).
  7: **Parameter Update:**
  8: Update the parameters of the student model: $\mathbf{W}^{(j,k)} \leftarrow \mathbf{W}^{(j,k)} - \eta \frac{\partial \mathcal{L}}{\partial \mathbf{W}^{(j,k)}}$, $\overline{W}^{(i,j,k)} \leftarrow \overline{W}^{(i,j,k)} - \eta \frac{\partial \mathcal{L}}{\partial \overline{W}^{(i,j,k)}}$.

---

is defined as follows:

$$\frac{\partial \mathcal{L}}{\partial y_t^{(j,k)}} = \frac{\partial \mathcal{L}}{\partial x_t^{(j,k+1)}} \frac{\partial x_t^{(j,k+1)}}{\partial y_t^{(j,k)}} + \sum_i^{i \neq j} \frac{\partial \mathcal{L}}{\partial x_t^{(i,k+1)}} \frac{\partial x_t^{(i,k+1)}}{\partial y_t^{(j,k)}}, \qquad (5.16)$$

where $y_t^{(j,k)}$ is the element of $Y_t^{(j,k)}$. We can observe that the gradient of the output features $y_t^{(j,k)}$ consists of the backward gradients from the self-subnet and other subnets. Then we bring Eq. (5.9) into Eq. (5.16), and the final backward gradient computation form can be rewritten as

$$\frac{\partial \mathcal{L}}{\partial y_t^{(j,k)}} = \frac{\partial \mathcal{L}}{\partial x_t^{(j,k+1)}} + \sum_i^{i \neq j} \overline{W}_t^{(j,i,k)} \frac{\partial \mathcal{L}}{\partial x_t^{(i,k+1)}}, \qquad (5.17)$$

where the gradient of $y_t^{(j,k)}$ is the sum of gradients from itself and the weighted sum of gradients from other subnets.

The CBN-Net attempts to explore the optimal lateral structure defined by the channelwise weight $\overline{W}_t^{(i,j,k)}$ for higher classification accuracy. To estimate the optimal weight $\overline{W}_t^{(i,j,k)}$ associated with the lateral connections, technically, its gradient can be calculated as follows:

$$\frac{\partial \mathcal{L}}{\partial \overline{W}_t^{(i,j,k)}} = \sum_{x_t^{(j,k+1)}} \frac{\partial \mathcal{L}}{\partial x_t^{(j,k+1)}} \frac{\partial x_t^{(j,k+1)}}{\partial \overline{W}_t^{(i,j,k)}}, \qquad (5.18)$$

where summation $\sum_{x_t^{(j,k+1)}}$ is applied to all entries in the tth channel, and the second term can be computed by Eq. (5.9). The key steps of the training process of our method are shown in Algorithm 5.1. With this novel binary network structure, we can train a highly accurate binary neural network in an end-to-end manner.

5.4 Application to efficient image classification

In this section, we conduct experiments with the proposed CBN-Net on two benchmark datasets, CIFAR-10 [23] and ILSVRC12 ImageNet [24]. Meanwhile, its classification performance was compared with other state-of-the-art binary neural networks.

5.4.1 Datasets and experiment settings

CIFAR-10. CIFAR-10 dataset [23] included 60,000 32×32 RGB color images, where there were totally 10 classes with 6000 images per class. There were 50,000 images used for training and 10,000 images used for testing the model performance. Similarly to previous works, we adopted the data augmentation strategies including random crop and flipping while tensor normalization was applied on both the training set and testing set.

ImageNet. ILSVRC 2012 ImageNet [24] was a large-scale dataset with 1000 classes, including 1.2 million high-resolution natural images for training and 50k images for testing. The most used data augmentation strategies such as random crop, flipping, and PCA noise were applied during training. In test time, we reported the evaluation results over 224 × 224 center-cropped testing images.

Implementation Details. All the experiments were implemented using PyTorch [25] and conducted on a single computer with 4 NVIDIA RTX 2080Ti GPUs.

For CIFAR-10 experiments, we chose ResNet-20 as the baseline model. During the training phase, the initial learning rate was 0.1, and the batch size was 128. The SGD optimizer with the momentum of 0.9

was used as the base optimizer, the weight decay was set as 1×10^{-4}, and the cosine annealing scheduler was adopted to adjust the learning rate. The teacher model used for knowledge distillation was using two ResNet-20 subnets with lateral connections.

For ImageNet experiments, we selected ResNet-18 as the baseline model and used ResNet-50 as the teacher model for knowledge distillation. Considering the limited computation resources, we only used two subnets to build the CBN-Net. The SGD optimizer with the momentum of 0.9 was adopted, the batch size was 256, and the weight decay was set to 0. We used the pretrained binary ResNet-18 to initialize each subnet in CBN-Net and fine-tuned the entire model for 45 epochs. The initial learning rate was set as 0.01 and multiplied by 0.1 at the 15th and 30th epochs, respectively.

5.4.2 Ablation test

A group of ablation test experiments was performed on the CIFAR-10 dataset to evaluate the effectiveness of the proposed CBN-Net. We used the binary Bireal-Net as the baseline model, which was based on the ResNet-20 backbone. We set the soft radio $\rho = 0.99$ and temperature $T = 5$ and trained all the models for 400 epochs.

Degenerate CBN-Net with no Lateral Connections: Firstly, we extended the baseline model, which had a single feed-forward pipeline, to a degenerate version of CBN-Net containing K subnets. The degenerate CBN-Net (NLC&NKD) with no lateral connections and no knowledge distillation was trained in an end-to-end manner. Fig. 5.4 compared the mean accuracy of the full-precision (FP) model, the binary baseline model, the Binary Ensemble Neural Network, and the CBN-Net (NLC&NKD). The degenerate CBN-Net (NLC&NKD) achieved 86.87% to 88.60% average accuracy when the number of the subnets changed from 2 to 6, which were consistently better than the compared methods; however, there was still an accuracy drop of roughly 3% compared with the full-precision model.

Effectiveness of Knowledge Distillation: Secondly, we improved the degenerate CBN-Net with two subnets by adopting the knowledge distillation loss function, and we evaluated the CBN-Net (NLC&KD) where its hyperparameter ρ was set to 0.99 and T was set to 5. The teacher model used for knowledge distillation was using two ResNet-20 subnets with lateral connections. Fig. 5.5 compared the accuracy growth curve of the CBN-Net (NLC&NKD) and CBN-Net (NLC&KD) with knowledge

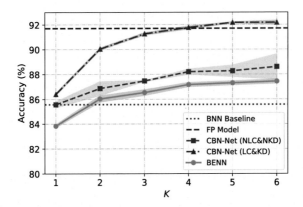

Figure 5.4 Accuracy of the BNN baseline, degenerate CBN-Net (NLC&NKD) with no lateral connections and no knowledge distillation, the BENN, the CBN-Net (LC&KD), and the full-precision model with respect to the number of subnets K on the CIFAR-10 dataset.

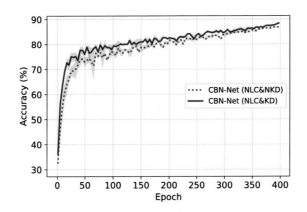

Figure 5.5 Accuracy of the degenerate CBN-Net (NLC&NKD) and the CBN-Net (NLC&KD) with knowledge distillation but no lateral connections on the CIFAR-10 dataset.

distillation. The CBN–Net (NLC&KD) benefited from the informative supervised signals of the teacher model and achieved roughly 1% validation accuracy in comparison with the CBN–Net (NLC&NKD) during the training process.

As demonstrated in Table 5.1, the CBN–Net (NLC&KD) achieved 88.53% mean accuracy on the CIFAR–10 dataset and improved the mean accuracy of the degenerate CBN–Net (NLC&NKD) by 1.32%.

Effectiveness of Lateral Connections: Thirdly, we further improved the degenerate CBN–Net by introducing the lateral connections between

Table 5.1 Summary of the ablation study on CIFAR-10, where K indicates the number of binary subnets, NLC means no lateral connections, NKD means no knowledge distillation. We run each model several times and report the "best (mean±std)" accuracy.

Method	K	γ	ρ	Acc(%)
FP Model	–	–	–	91.7 (best)
BNN Baseline	1	–	–	85.55 (85.48±0.10)
CBN-Net (NLC&NKD)	2	0	0	87.36 (87.21±0.12)
CBN-Net (NLC&KD)	2	0	0.99	88.73 (88.53±0.14)
CBN-Net (LC&KD)	2	10^{-4}	0.99	90.14 (90.05±0.09)
CBN-Net (LC&KD)	5	10^{-4}	0.99	**92.21** (92.19±0.01)

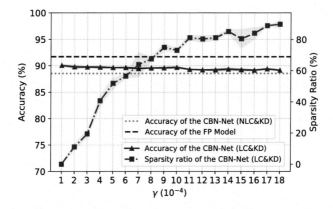

Figure 5.6 Accuracy and sparsity ratio of the CBN-Net (LC&KD) with both lateral connections and knowledge distillation *w.r.t.* the regularization coefficient γ on the CIFAR-10 dataset.

two binary subnets to build the proposed CBN-Net (LC&KD). Fig. 5.6 demonstrated the *sparsity ratio* and validation accuracy of the CBN-Net (LC&KD) with various regularization coefficients γ, where the sparsity ratio represented the ratio of the lateral connections with near–zero lateral weights. The mean sparsity ratio of the lateral connections increased from 0% to 89.83% when γ varied from 1.0×10^{-4} to 1.8×10^{-3}; however, the mean accuracy of the model was nearly unchanged around 90%, which meant that roughly over 80% of lateral connections were redundant for accurate classification. Besides, it could be seen that the CBN-Net (LC&KD) may degenerate to the CBN-Net (NLC&KD) when the regularization coefficient γ went even larger than 1.8×10^{-3}, which meant that all the lateral connections were pruned off during the learning process.

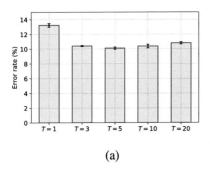 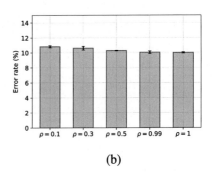

(a)   (b)

Figure 5.7 (a) Error rate of the CBN-Net (LC&KD) with respect to different temperatures T when $\rho = 0.99$. (b) Error rate of the CBN-Net (LC&KD) with respect to different soft ratios ρ when $T = 5$.

Though the CBN-Net learned from the full-precision model by knowledge distillation, surprisingly, it could outperform the full-precision baseline when a few more subnets were added. As shown in Fig. 5.4, the mean accuracy of the CBN-Net (LC&KD) surpassed the full-precision ResNet-20 when K was larger than 4. Detailed results were in Table 5.1; the CBN-Net (LC&KD) with five subnets achieved 92.19% mean accuracy, which was higher than the full-precision ResNet-20 (91.7%).

Analysis of Hyper-parameters: Finally, we evaluated the CBN-Net (LC&KD) with two subnets and various hyperparameters of soft ratio ρ and temperature T. We fixed the regularization coefficient $\gamma = 1.0 \times 10^{-4}$ in these experiments.

As shown in Fig. 5.7, we first fixed $\rho = 0.99$ and tuned T in the range of 1 to 20 to see the influence of T. The lowest mean error rate 10.08% was achieved when $T = 5$, which reduced the shift of output distribution caused by binary quantization. The highest mean error rate was obtained when $T = 1$, which indicated that the softened probabilities were useful for knowledge distillation in BNNs.

On the other hand, we fixed T as 5 and tuned ρ in the range of 0.1 to 1.0 to analyze the effect of ρ. The highest error rate 10.80% was obtained when $\rho = 0.1$, which meant that, potentially, the KL loss was more important than the CE loss. Therefore we recommended to use a large value of the soft ratio, e.g., $\rho = 0.99$, for better performance, which was coherent with [26].

Comparison with SOTA on CIFAR-10: Table 5.2 compared the CBN-Net with other state-of-the-art binary neural networks such as DoReFa [14], DSQ [27], IR-Net [28], RBNN [29] based on ResNet-20,

Table 5.2 Classification performance compared with the SOTA methods on CIFAR-10. We run the training process several times for our method and report the "best (mean±std)" accuracy.

Topology	Method	W/A	Acc(%)
ResNet20	FP Model	32/32	91.7 (best)
	DoReFa	1/1	79.3 (best)
	DSQ	1/1	84.1 (best)
	IR-Net	1/1	86.5 (best)
	RBNN	1/1	87.8 (best)
	CBN-Net ($K=2$)	1/1	90.14 (90.05±0.09)
	CBN-Net ($K=5$)	1/1	**92.21** (92.19±0.01)
VGG-Small	FP Model	32/32	91.7 (best)
	LAB	1/1	87.7 (best)
	XNOR	1/1	89.8 (best)
	BinaryNet	1/1	89.9 (best)
	IR-Net	1/1	90.4 (best)
	RBNN	1/1	91.3 (best)
	CBN-Net ($K=2$)	1/1	**92.97** (92.77±0.17)

and LAB [30], XNOR, BinaryNet, IR-Net, and RBNN based on VGG-Small. We clearly see that the proposed CBN-Net outperformed other state-of-the-art BNNs by a relatively large margin and achieved higher classification accuracy than the full-precision models with both ResNet-20 (92.21%) and VGG-Small (92.97%) backbones.

5.4.3 Experiments on ImageNet

We validated the proposed method on the large-scale ImageNet dataset. Table 5.3 listed other state-of-the-art BNNs including BWN [10], XNOR, BinaryNet, DoReFa-Net, HWGQ [31], TBN [32], Quantization Networks [33], Bireal-Net, XNOR++ [34], Bop [35], IR-Net, RBNN, LNS [36], and ReActNet [37].

All the compared methods in Table 5.3 were based on the same binary configuration of the backbone ResNet-18. We used the pretrained parameters of the ReActNet [37] for the CBN-Net initialization. As shown in Table 5.3, the best Top-1 accuracy (66.8%) of the proposed CBN-Net was higher than other state-of-the-art binary neural networks with binary weights and activations. It was interesting to find out that the CBN-Net even outperformed some quantized models including HWGQ and TBN, which adopted representation with higher precision.

Table 5.3 Accuracy comparison with the SOTA methods on the ImageNet dataset. "W" and "A" refer to the bit width of weights and activations, respectively.

Method	Year	W/A	Top-1
ResNet18	2016	32/32	69.6%
BWN	2016	1/32	60.8%
BinaryNet	2016	1/1	42.2%
DoReFa-Net	2016	1/1	52.5%
XNOR-Net	2016	1/1	51.2%
HWGQ	2017	1/2	59.6%
TBN	2018	1/2	55.6%
Bireal-Net	2018	1/1	56.4%
XNOR++	2019	1/1	57.1%
Quantization Networks	2019	1/1	53.6%
Bop	2019	1/1	54.2%
IR-Net	2020	1/1	58.1%
LNS	2020	1/1	59.4%
RBNN	2020	1/1	59.9%
ReActNet	2020	1/1	65.9%
CBN-Net $(K=2)$	2021	1/1	**66.8%**

5.4.4 Complexity analysis

We evaluated the computational complexity of the proposed CBN-Net on the ImageNet dataset and compared it with other binary neural networks. Table 5.4 lists the state-of-the-art BNNs with over 60% Top-1 accuracy on the ImageNet dataset, including ABC-Net, BENN, Group-Net, and the Circulant BNN [16]. These methods generally made a trade-off between efficiency and accuracy, and used multiple subnets or bases of binary matrices to reduce the drop of classification accuracy.

The computational complexity was measured by the total operations (OPs), which consisted of floating-point operations and binary operations, and we used the same OPs estimation procedure as [37]. In summary, the CBN-Net achieved the 1.8% to 5.7% higher Top-1 classification accuracy compared to these methods. Moreover, the CBN-Net was the most efficient method in terms of inference OPs compared to the state-of-the-art binary neural networks. It was worth noting that even containing two subnets, the CBN-Net was still 5.58× to 8.62× more efficient than the full-precision network due to its binary representation and binary operation.

Table 5.4 Complexity comparison with the SOTA methods on the ImageNet dataset.

Method	Year	Weights bit × number	Activations bit × number	Memory Mbit	OPs MOPs	Top-1
ResNet-18	2016	32	32	374	1810	69.6%
ABC-Net	2017	1 × 5	1 × 5	88.45	300.06	65.0%
BENN	2019	1 × 6	1 × 6	201.94	983.91	61.1%
Group-Net	2019	1 × 4	1 × 4	85.43	654.51	64.2%
Circulant BNN	2020	1 × 4	1 × 4	**66.58**	242.56	61.4%
CBN-Net ($K=2$)	2021	1 × 2	1 × 2	67.02	**209.97**	**66.8%**

References

[1] S. Han, H. Mao, W.J. Dally, Deep compression: Compressing deep neural networks with pruning, trained quantization and Huffman coding, in: Proceedings of International Conference on Learning Representations, 2015, pp. 1–14.

[2] E.L. Denton, W. Zaremba, J. Bruna, Y. LeCun, R. Fergus, Exploiting linear structure within convolutional networks for efficient evaluation, in: Proceedings of International Conference on Neural Information Processing Systems, 2014, pp. 1269–1277.

[3] X. Zhang, X. Zhou, M. Lin, J. Sun, ShuffleNet: An extremely efficient convolutional neural network for mobile devices, in: Proceedings of the IEEE Conference on Computer Vision and Pattern Recognition, 2018, pp. 6848–6856.

[4] M. Tan, Q.V. Le, EfficientNet: Rethinking model scaling for convolutional neural networks, arXiv:1905.11946 [abs].

[5] G. Hinton, O. Vinyals, J. Dean, Distilling the knowledge in a neural network, in: Proceedings of International Conference on Neural Information Processing Systems, 2014, pp. 1–9.

[6] S. Gupta, A. Agrawal, K. Gopalakrishnan, P. Narayanan, Deep learning with limited numerical precision, in: Proceedings of International Conference on Machine Learning, 2015, pp. 1737–1746.

[7] I. Hubara, M. Courbariaux, D. Soudry, R. El-Yaniv, Y. Bengio, Binarized neural networks, in: Proceedings of International Conference on Neural Information Processing Systems, 2016, pp. 4107–4115.

[8] X. Zhou, K. Liu, C. Shi, H. Liu, J. Liu, Neural network activation quantization with bitwise information bottlenecks, arXiv:2006.05210 [abs].

[9] X. Zhou, Y. Peng, C. Long, F. Ren, C. Shi, MoNet3D: Towards accurate monocular 3D object localization in real time, in: Proceedings of International Conference on Machine Learning, 2020, pp. 11503–11512.

[10] M. Rastegari, V. Ordonez, J. Redmon, A. Farhadi, XNOR-Net: ImageNet classification using binary convolutional neural networks, in: Proceedings of European Conference on Computer Vision, 2016, pp. 525–542.

[11] X. Lin, C. Zhao, W. Pan, Towards accurate binary convolutional neural network, in: Proceedings of International Conference on Neural Information Processing Systems, 2017, pp. 345–353.

[12] B. Zhuang, C. Shen, M. Tan, L. Liu, I. Reid, Structured binary neural networks for accurate image classification and semantic segmentation, in: Proceedings of IEEE Conference on Computer Vision and Pattern Recognition, 2019, pp. 413–422.

[13] S. Zhu, X. Dong, H. Su, Binary ensemble neural network: More bits per network or more networks per bit?, in: Proceedings of IEEE Conference on Computer Vision and Pattern Recognition, 2019, pp. 4923–4932.

[14] S. Zhou, Y. Wu, Z. Ni, X. Zhou, H. Wen, Y. Zou, DoReFa-Net: Training low bitwidth convolutional neural networks with low bitwidth gradients, arXiv:1606.06160 [abs].

[15] Z. Liu, B. Wu, W. Luo, X. Yang, W. Liu, K.-T. Cheng, Bi-real net: Enhancing the performance of 1-bit CNNS with improved representational capability and advanced training algorithm, in: Proceedings of European Conference on Computer Vision, 2018, pp. 722–737.

[16] C. Liu, W. Ding, X. Xia, B. Zhang, J. Gu, J. Liu, R. Ji, D. Doermann, Circulant binary convolutional networks: Enhancing the performance of 1-bit DCNNs with circulant back propagation, in: Proceedings of IEEE Conference on Computer Vision and Pattern Recognition, 2019, pp. 2691–2699.

[17] H. Qin, R. Gong, X. Liu, X. Bai, J. Song, N. Sebe, Binary neural networks: A survey, Pattern Recognition 105 (2020) 107281.

[18] M. Wilms, S.B. Eickhoff, L. Hömke, C. Rottschy, M. Kujovic, K. Amunts, G.R. Fink, Comparison of functional and cytoarchitectonic maps of human visual areas V1, V2, V3d, V3v, and V4(v), NeuroImage 49 (2) (2010) 1171–1179.

[19] N. Milosevic, D. Ristanovic, Fractality of dendritic arborization of spinal cord neurons, Neuroscience Letters 396 (3) (2006) 172–176.

[20] K. Friston, Learning and inference in the brain, Neural Networks 16 (9) (2003) 1325–1352.

[21] Y. Bengio, N. Leonard, A. Courville, Estimating or propagating gradients through stochastic neurons for conditional computation, arXiv:1308.3432 [abs].

[22] J. Bethge, C. Bartz, H. Yang, Y. Chen, C. Meinel, MeliusNet: Can binary neural networks achieve MobileNet-level accuracy?, arXiv:2001.05936 [abs].

[23] A. Krizhevsky, G. Hinton, et al., Learning multiple layers of features from tiny images, Technical report, 2009.

[24] J. Deng, W. Dong, R. Socher, L.-J. Li, K. Li, L. Fei-Fei, ImageNet: A large-scale hierarchical image database, in: Proceedings of IEEE Conference on Computer Vision and Pattern Recognition, 2009, pp. 248–255.

[25] A. Paszke, S. Gross, F. Massa, A. Lerer, J. Bradbury, G. Chanan, T. Killeen, Z. Lin, N. Gimelshein, L. Antiga, et al., PyTorch: An imperative style, high-performance deep learning library, in: Proceedings of International Conference on Neural Information Processing Systems, 2019, pp. 8026–8037.

[26] G. Ji, Z. Zhu, Knowledge distillation in wide neural networks: Risk bound, data efficiency and imperfect teacher, arXiv:2010.10090 [abs].

[27] R. Gong, X. Liu, S. Jiang, T. Li, P. Hu, J. Lin, F. Yu, J. Yan, Differentiable soft quantization: Bridging full-precision and low-bit neural networks, in: Proceedings of IEEE International Conference on Computer Vision, 2019, pp. 4852–4861.

[28] H. Qin, R. Gong, X. Liu, M. Shen, Z. Wei, F. Yu, J. Song, Forward and backward information retention for accurate binary neural networks, in: Proceedings of IEEE Conference on Computer Vision and Pattern Recognition, 2020, pp. 2250–2259.

[29] M. Lin, R. Ji, Z. Xu, B. Zhang, Y. Wang, Y. Wu, F. Huang, C.-W. Lin, Rotated binary neural network, in: Proceedings of International Conference on Neural Information Processing Systems, 2020, pp. 1–12.

[30] L. Hou, Q. Yao, J.T. Kwok, Loss-aware binarization of deep networks, in: Proceedings of International Conference on Learning Representations, 2016, pp. 1–11.

[31] Z. Cai, X. He, J. Sun, N. Vasconcelos, Deep learning with low precision by half-wave Gaussian quantization, in: Proceedings of IEEE Conference on Computer Vision and Pattern Recognition, 2017, pp. 5918–5926.

[32] D. Wan, F. Shen, L. Liu, F. Zhu, J. Qin, L. Shao, H. Tao Shen, TBN: Convolutional neural network with ternary inputs and binary weights, in: Proceedings of European Conference on Computer Vision, 2018, pp. 315–332.

[33] J. Yang, X. Shen, J. Xing, X. Tian, H. Li, B. Deng, J. Huang, X.-s. Hua, Quantization networks, in: Proceedings of IEEE Conference on Computer Vision and Pattern Recognition, 2019, pp. 7308–7316.

[34] A. Bulat, G. Tzimiropoulos, XNOR-Net++: Improved binary neural networks, in: Proceedings of British Machine Vision Conference, 2019, pp. 1–12.

[35] K. Helwegen, J. Widdicombe, L. Geiger, Z. Liu, K.-T. Cheng, R. Nusselder, Latent weights do not exist: Rethinking binarized neural network optimization, in: Proceedings of International Conference on Neural Information Processing Systems, 2019, pp. 7533–7544.

[36] K. Han, Y. Wang, Y. Xu, C. Xu, E. Wu, C. Xu, Training binary neural networks through learning with noisy supervision, in: Proceedings of International Conference on Machine Learning, 2020, pp. 4017–4026.

[37] Z. Liu, Z. Shen, M. Savvides, K.-T. Cheng, ReActNet: Towards precise binary neural network with generalized activation functions, in: Proceedings of European Conference on Computer Vision, 2020.

PART 3

Architecture optimization

CHAPTER 6

Binary neural network computing architecture

6.1 Background and challenges

This chapter is based on our related publication [1]. The past several years have witnessed a sharp increase in the applications of convolutional neural networks (CNNs), which are very suitable for various deep learning tasks, especially for computer vision [2–4]. However, it cannot be deployed on mobile platforms conveniently due to the limit of high computation complexity and huge network model size. To overcome these problems, by leveraging neural network compression techniques, we can reduce the size of neural networks and improve the computation speed. As an extreme solution of compressed neural network, binary neural networks (BNNs) were first proposed by Courbariaux and Bengio [5] in 2016.

BNN constrains both weights and activations to $+1$ and -1, which can tremendously reduce the model size of traditional full precision CNN by $32\times$. It brings great convenience to the implementation of hardware on low power dissipation and memory requirement. Based on these advantages, several hardware accelerators of BNN have been proposed. A BNN accelerator in [6] opens up the study of FPGA acceleration for BNNs and explores an HLS heterogeneous methodology to maximize the system throughout. FINN is proposed in [7], which is a framework for using a flexible heterogeneous architecture to build fast and flexible FPGA accelerators. A framework in [8] is proposed as the first fully binarized neural network accelerator architecture, in which all layers are binarized. These works show very promising performance and energy efficiency.

However, in their works, model performance can only be guaranteed by complex network models, which results in large memory footprint and power consumption, and more promising optimization on reducing hardware memory costs of BNN is absent. In this chapter the ensemble technique for BNN is introduced to hardware implementation. Based on bagging ensemble method, the bagged binary neural network accelerator (BBNA) is introduced, which is a fully pipelined BNN accelerator with bagging unit for aggregating several BNNs to achieve better model accuracy, i.e., a smaller network can make it more accurate than a network much

Deep Learning on Edge Computing Devices
https://doi.org/10.1016/B978-0-32-385783-3.00015-6

larger than itself. This means that we can deploy a smaller network model on memory-limited embedded devices with similar accuracy as a bigger one for dramatically saving memory. BBNA designs a bagging PE to support different aggregation methods of BNNs. The highly parallel processing element has flexible data-stream architecture for different feature map sizes. BBNA uses pipelines to improve data throughput and processing speed of overall system. The BBNA was implemented based FPGA prototypes on a Stratix-V GXA7 FPGA platform. It can achieve high performance with ultralow memory cost and power consumption. Finally, a BBNA-based prototype system demonstration was designed on DE5-net board to demonstrate its practicability and usability.

6.2 Ensemble binary neural computing model

6.2.1 Convolutional neural network

The model structure of a typical convolutional neural network (CNN) [9] is given in Fig. 6.1. CNN is a multilevel structure with trainable parameters, in which the input and output of each level are composed of a set of two-dimensional vectors, which are called feature maps (fmaps). In a CNN, each output feature map (ofmap) represents some feature information extracted from the input feature map (ifmap). Commonly, each level structure of typical CNN is orderly composed of a CONV or fully connection (FC) layer, a batch normalization (BN) layer, an activation layer, and a pooling layer if necessary.

The input and output of the CONV layer are a set of feature maps, each containing different feature information, which use a set of trained filters to convolve the ifmaps through multiplication and accumulation (MAC) operations between filters and the pixels at the corresponding position of ifmap in a sliding-window way with a stride. The pooling layer can be

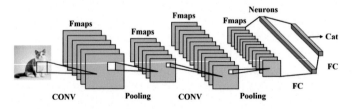

Figure 6.1 Model Structure of a typical CNN, always including input, multiple convolutional (CONV) and pooling layers, fully connection (FC) layers, and output.

viewed as a down-sampling process that reduces the data dimension. The FC layer performs a liner transformation between the weights and 1-D vectors formed from the final CONV layer by a flatten way. A network with only FC layers commonly can be called a multilayer perceptron (MLP).

CONV operation is generally followed by BN operation, which can normalize the distribution of input of each layer to reduce the training time and improve the generalization ability of the network. Then the activation function comes closely after BN, which introduces the ability to fit nonlinearity to network through some special functions such as ReLU, sigmoid, etc.

6.2.2 Binary neural network

Complex CNN can extract complex feature information for difficult machine learning tasks. Nevertheless, the more complex the network model, the more difficult the deploying it on an embedded mobile device due to the huge memory and power consumption. The binary neural network (BNN) is the most extreme scheme that constrains both weights and activations to ± 1, and its quantification method is implemented as either probabilistic or deterministic sign function [5].

To store weights within only 1 bit on hardware, we convert -1 to 0 and 1 to 1 by affine transformation, respectively, which can transform MAC operations to XNOR and popcount operations, i.e., performing bitwise XNOR between weights and inputs, and counting the number of 1s in the intermediate result after XNOR operation. The convolution of BNN is formulated as

$$\mathbf{Y} = \mathbf{B}_x \otimes \mathbf{B}_w + \boldsymbol{b}, \tag{6.1}$$

where $\otimes$ indicates XNOR-POPCOUNT operation, $\mathbf{B}_x$ is the binary input, $\mathbf{B}_w$ is a binary weight associated with that input, and $\boldsymbol{b}$ is the neuron bias.

The BN operation and binarized activation function come closely after CONV layer. The sign activation function of BNN [5] is defined as

$$\mathbf{B}_y = \text{sign}(\mathbf{Y}) = \begin{cases} +1, & \mathbf{Y} \geq 0, \\ -1, & \mathbf{Y} < 0. \end{cases} \tag{6.2}$$

This implies that we only need to take out the sign bit of the intermediate result to implement the nonlinear activation. Further, we combine

BN and activation for facilitating hardware implementation, which can be expressed as

$$\mathbf{B_y} = \text{sign}(\mathbf{Y}_{bn}) = \text{sign}\left(\gamma\left(\frac{\mathbf{Y}-\mu}{\sigma}\right)+\beta\right), \qquad (6.3)$$

where the $\mathbf{Y}_{bn}$ denotes the output of BN layer according to [10]. Equation (6.3) is equivalent to the following expression:

$$\mathbf{B_y} = \text{sign}\left(\frac{\gamma}{\sigma}\left(\mathbf{Y}+\left(-\mu+\frac{\sigma}{\gamma}\beta\right)\right)\right), \qquad (6.4)$$

where μ and σ are the mean value and standard deviation of each minibatch (i.e., output of CONV layer), and γ and β are the scaling and shifting factors that can be trained. Interestingly, γ and σ are positive constants in the inference phase, so we just need to calculate the integer bias $(-\mu + (\sigma/\gamma)\beta)$ after training, so that we only adopt an adder to complete the BN and activation operations.

6.2.3 Ensemble binary neural network

Since the ultralow algorithm complexity and memory requirement, BNNs open a new window for allowing more mobile devices to share the benefits of the rise of deep learning. However, BNNs with 1-bit weights and activations suffer from grievous drop in accuracy due to their weak representation ability. To improve the model performance, Zhu et al. [11] presented a binary ensemble neural network (BENN), which aggregates multiple single-bit BNNs to obtain a better performance than a multibit quantization network in ensemble learning ways, including bagging and boosting. The BENN has also significantly enhanced the intrinsic stability and robustness of original weak BNN, which are primarily reflected in the large fluctuation of training accuracy and model overfitting problem, respectively.

The bagging method is introduced into our hardware architecture; the schematic diagram of BNN with bagging is illustrated in Fig. 6.2. To follow the bootstrapping principle of bagging [12], M training samples of each BNN classifier are randomly sampled with replacement from the total training set D, which are assumed to be independent identically distributed samples. Then we can get K weak BNN classifiers after K independent trainings. In the inference phase, we use two different voting mechanisms

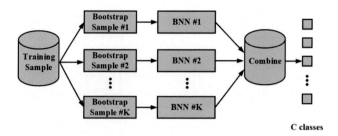

Figure 6.2 Schematic diagram of bagged BNN. *K* independent BNN classifiers are trained based on different training samples to obtain *K* weak classifiers, which are then combined to form the final classifier.

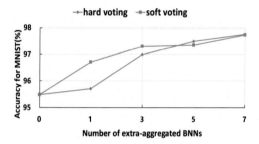

Figure 6.3 The accuracy of 64-128-128 BMLP model on MNIST when we change the number of extra-aggregated BNNs based on one BNN.

to combine the opinions of K BNN classifiers for obtaining the final classification label. One is the hard voting, which selects the majority agreed label as the final label, and the other is selecting the best label after averaging the softmax probability of all classifiers, which be called soft voting.

We evaluated the bagging method on 64-128-128 bagged MLP (BMLP), which is a three-layer fully connected neural network for MNIST handwriting dataset, and each layer has 128 neurons except the first layer, which has 64. We compared two voting methods with different number of aggregated BNNs in terms of model accuracy. As shown in Fig. 6.3, the model with soft voting is always more accurate than that with hard voting, and the accuracy increases from 95.5% to 97.7% when we aggregate extra BNNs from 0 to 7. Interestingly, the situation was quite opposite when we applied the bagging method to some other model, so our hardware architecture supports both hard and soft voting to meet various task requirements with different networks.

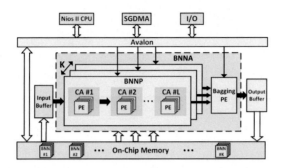

Figure 6.4 The overall system architecture.

6.3 Architecture design and optimization

6.3.1 Overall architecture

As illustrated in Fig. 6.4, a data-stream-based architecture was adopted in BBNA, which mainly consists of K independent BNN pipelines (BNNPs) and bagging PE. Each BNNP performs the operation of one ensemble BNN. Bagging PE is responsible for aggregating the outputs of K BNNPs in the inference phase. Considering resource utilization efficiency and power consumption, we implemented bagging by the aggregate of multiple parallel BNNPs instead of the reuse of one BNNP, which loads the parameters of different ensemble BNNs at once from the on-chip memory in every inference time and combines all outputs after all the inferences are completed.

Each BNNP has several computing arrays (CAs) with multiple processing elements (PEs). Each CA is dedicated to the corresponding macrolayer of BNN, which cascaded through high-speed Avalon Streaming (Avalon-ST) bus. NIOS II processor is used to flexibly configure the architecture of all CAs and control them via the Avalon Memory Mapping (Avalon-MM) interface. The parameters and intermediate results of all BNNs are stored in the on-chip memory, which can eliminate off-chip memory accesses to extremely save power consumption and improve throughput.

On the other hand, the I/O peripherals (e.g., universal asynchronous receiver/transmitter (UART)) mounted on the Avalon Bus can help us build a BBNA-based prototype system. Additionally, we can utilize the Scatter-gather DMA (SGDMA) IP core to complete high-speed input data handling, convert the data format of the input data into that required high-speed I/O devices, and also improve the work efficiency of CPU.

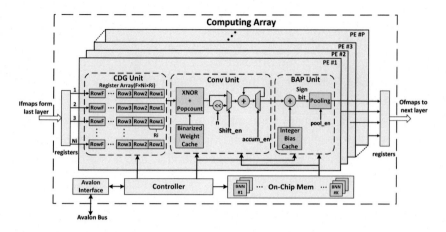

Figure 6.5 Block diagram of CA and PE.

6.3.2 Architecture of computing array

The internal block diagram of CA is shown in Fig. 6.5. A fully pipelined data path organization between all submodules is adopted to reduce the path delay and enhance the processing throughput. At the same time, our accelerator has many designs for achieving universality and configurability. The calculation of each layer is controlled by the controller which is connected to the Avalon Bus via an Avalon interface. Different PEs load the same ifmaps from the output register buffer of last layer in a ping-pong way and calculate the ofmap for each independent channel, and then write the intermediate results to the register buffer for the next computation.

The core component of CA is multiple highly paralleled P PE units, which are responsible for the computation of C/F layer of BNN. The PE has several parts: Calculated Data Generator (CDG) unit, Convolution (Conv) Unit, and Batch Normalization, Activation, and Pooling (BAP) unit. The CDG unit is used for caching and generating the calculation data required by the subsequent Conv unit. It is composed of N_i shift register buffers corresponding to the channels of ifmaps, and each buffer contains sequential F rows of length R_i. To increase the reconfigurability, we design both F and N_i as configurable parameters, and the R_i can also be configured according to the ifmap size of each layer. The number of rows F is commonly equal to the size of convolution kernel, so if a streaming architecture is adopted, which pushes pixel data into register buffer per clock, then we can fetch the data to the Conv unit per clock once F rows of ifmaps arrive. Otherwise, if the architecture is not streaming, then we can also load F rows of ifmaps from the intermediate cache per clock. In this case, we can further increase R_i to improve the system bandwidth. For example, in the first cycle, we can set R_i to 56 when F is 3 and the size of ifmap is 28×28; the first six lines of ifmaps are required to calculate the first four lines of ofmaps, so that it increases the bandwidth twice as much as when R_i is 28. For FC layer, we simply flatten register buffers into a one-dimensional vector and feed it into the Conv unit.

BNN maps the original MAC operations of convolution to XNOR and Popcount operation. The Popcount operation depends on the 6-input 3-output look-up table (LUT), which suitably fits the FPGA resources. The results of XNOR and Popcount module are used as the input of the following shifter and accumulator. Accumulator is needed because the PE cannot always finish computing once for arbitrary network model. Besides, PE with shifter and accumulator can meet the case of multibit calculation such as the first layer of network, which is usually a multibit RGB image, because the shifter is able to realize n shifts according to the bit weight of a binary. It is also suitable for other neural networks adopting various bit-width quantization strategies. Subsequently, the BN and binarized activation are accomplished by integer addition and taking out the sign bit. Finally, the activation outputs flow into pooling unit, which transforms the max pooling operation into Boolean OR operations because the activation values are 0 or 1 only.

6.3.3 Bagging processing element

The architecture of bagging PE is illustrated in Fig. 6.6, which consists of hard voting (HV) and soft voting (SV) units. HV unit is used to count the respective votes of C labels. The softmax classifier orderly classifies BNN outputs, denoted 01, ..., 0c, to get the best label, and then the controller activates the accumulator corresponding to the label. Specifically, to avoid labels that have the same votes, the input of the accumulator is the weight we assign to each classifier based on its performance rather than 1. Finally, the comparator chooses the label that has the most votes as the final label, whereas SV unit operates directly on the original outputs of BNNs and calculates the mean value of each label after K accumulations.

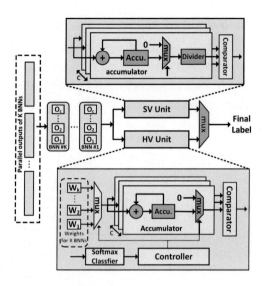

Figure 6.6 Architecture of bagging PE.

6.4 Application of binary computing architecture

6.4.1 Experiment setting

To better evaluate BBNA architecture, in addition to the 64-128-128 BMLP network we mentioned earlier, we also used one BNNP to implement a small binary CNN (BCNN) without bagging, which has two CONV layers with 32 and 64 convolution filters and an FC layer with 128 neurons. All CONV layers apply a structure in an order of C-B-A-P (CONV, BN, Activation, Pooling) and have 5×5 filters. The benchmarks for both models are MNIST handwriting datasets consisting of 60 K 28×28 gray images for training and 10 K images for testing [2]. The BBNA-BMLP we deployed on hardware aggregates eight BNNPs and uses hard voting, which has only 0.61 Mbit parameters and 1.22 M operations and achieves 97.7% accuracy. The BBNA-BCNN has more complex network with 21.74 M operations and 0.45 Mbit parameters, and it achieves over 99.2% accuracy.

We implemented FPGA-based prototypes of both models on the DE5-net board with an Intel Stratix-V GXA7 FPGA. Both models are implemented with Verilog HDL and synthesized, placed, and routed by Intel Quartus Prime 17.1, and used TimeQuest Timing Analyzer tool to constrain the system clock to 200 MHz. We used a power meter to measure the power consumption of boards.

6.4.2 Performance evaluation and comparison

As shown in Table 6.1, we compared the BBNA architecture with two common platforms and two FPGA based BNN accelerators. Two common platforms are Intel 8700K CPU and NVIDIA GTX2080Ti GPU, and both run the same Lenet network as our BBNA on MNIST. Then we compared our architecture with the LFC-max of FINN [7], which is a 1024-1024-1024 binarized MLP, and the MLP MNIST of FP-BNN [13], which has same number of layers, but each layer has 2048 neurons.

Although with an order of magnitude lower power and slower clock, BBNA-BCNN still results in about 89× and 1.4× better performance over CPU and GPU, respectively. Besides, it achieves 620× and 26× better in power efficiency over CPU and GPU, respectively.

Compared with the LFC-max of FINN [7], our BBNA-BMLP save 79% memory footprint with a negligible reduction in accuracy in the case where we all use the MLP model, thanks to the improvement of model performance brought by ensemble method, which is a boon for memory-limited devices. Besides, our models outperform FINN in energy efficiency.

The MLP MNIST design of FP-BNN [13] is implemented with a high-cost Stratix-V FPGA platform, which is similar to ours. With a similar accuracy on MNIST, our BBNA-BMLP achieves better performance and has a significant save of memory cost more than 94%. Due to better model performance of CNN, BBNA-BCNN has a higher accuracy. Moreover, our models achieve about 1.9× better energy efficiency due to lower memory footprint.

6.4.3 Prototype system demonstration

Fig. 6.7 shows our prototype system demonstration, which is composed of PC host computer and FPGA slave computer, and two computers communicate and transmit data through an RS-232 serial port. We can send any number of MNIST images to the FPGA through the graphical user interface (GUI) implemented by the PyQt5 frame. Then NIOS II CPU converts these pictures into data streams that conform to the protocol of Avalon-ST and send them to the BBNA for accelerating the computation. After the calculation is complete, CPU can take out the results by interrupt and return them to PC. This demo shows the practicability and usability of our design.

Table 6.1 Comparison with other BNN platforms.

Platform	Device	Clock (MHz)	Dataset	Accuracy (%)	Memory (Mbit)	Performance (GOPS)	Energy Efficiency (GOPS/W)
CPU	Intel i7-8700k	3.7k	MNIST	99.3	–	62	0.71
GPU	Nvidia GTX2080 Ti	1.35k	MNIST	99.3	–	3861	17
FINN [7]	Zynq XC7Z045	200	MNIST	98.4	2.9	9086	402
FP-BNN [8]	Stratix-V 5SGSD8	150	MNIST	98.2	10.01	5905	225
BBNA–BMLP	Stratix-V 5SGXMA7	200	MNIST	97.7	0.61	7373	424
BBNA–Lenet	Stratix-V 5SGXMA7	200	MNIST	99.2	0.56	5546	430

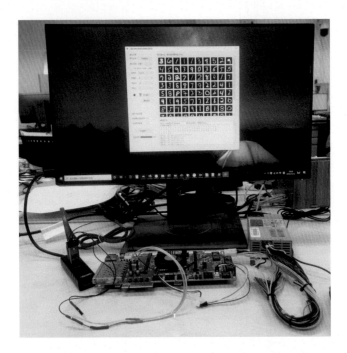

Figure 6.7 Prototype system demonstration.

References

[1] S. Liang, Y. Lin, W. He, L. Zhang, M. Wu, X. Zhou, An energy-efficient bagged binary neural network accelerator, in: Proceedings of IEEE 3rd International Conference on Electronics Technology, 2020, pp. 174–179.

[2] Y. LeCun, L. Bottou, Y. Bengio, P. Haffner, Gradient-based learning applied to document recognition, Proceedings of the IEEE 86 (11) (1998) 2278–2324.

[3] A. Krizhevsky, I. Sutskever, G.E. Hinton, ImageNet classification with deep convolutional neural networks, in: Proceedings of International Conference on Neural Information Processing Systems, vol. 25, 2012, pp. 1097–1105.

[4] A. Loquercio, A.I. Maqueda, C.R. Del-Blanco, D. Scaramuzza, DroNet: Learning to fly by driving, IEEE Robotics and Automation Letters 3 (2) (2018) 1088–1095.

[5] M. Courbariaux, I. Hubara, D. Soudry, R. El-Yaniv, Y. Bengio, Binarized neural networks: Training deep neural networks with weights and activations constrained to +1 or −1, arXiv:1602.02830 [abs].

[6] R. Zhao, W. Song, W. Zhang, T. Xing, J.-H. Lin, M. Srivastava, R. Gupta, Z. Zhang, Accelerating binarized convolutional neural networks with software-programmable FPGAs, in: Proceedings of ACM/SIGDA International Symposium on Field-Programmable Gate Arrays, 2017, pp. 15–24.

[7] Y. Umuroglu, N.J. Fraser, G. Gambardella, M. Blott, P. Leong, M. Jahre, K. Vissers, FINN: A framework for fast, scalable binarized neural network inference, in: Proceedings of ACM/SIGDA International Symposium on Field-Programmable Gate Arrays, 2017, pp. 65–74.

[8] P. Guo, H. Ma, R. Chen, P. Li, S. Xie, D. Wang, FBNA: A fully binarized neural network accelerator, in: Proceedings of International Conference on Field Programmable Logic and Applications, 2018, pp. 51–513.

[9] W. Liu, Z. Wang, X. Liu, N. Zeng, Y. Liu, F.E. Alsaadi, A survey of deep neural network architectures and their applications, Neurocomputing 234 (2017) 11–26.

[10] H. Yonekawa, H. Nakahara, On-chip memory based binarized convolutional deep neural network applying batch normalization free technique on an FPGA, in: Proceedings of IEEE International Parallel and Distributed Processing Symposium Workshops, 2017, pp. 98–105.

[11] S. Zhu, X. Dong, H. Su, Binary ensemble neural network: More bits per network or more networks per bit?, in: Proceedings of IEEE Conference on Computer Vision and Pattern Recognition, 2019, pp. 4923–4932.

[12] L. Breiman, Bagging predictors, Machine Learning 24 (2) (1996) 123–140.

[13] S. Liang, S. Yin, L. Liu, W. Luk, S. Wei, FP-BNN: Binarized neural network on FPGA, Neurocomputing 275 (2018) 1072–1086.

CHAPTER 7

Algorithm and hardware codesign of sparse binary network on-chip

7.1 Background and challenges

This chapter is based on our related publication [1]. The deep neural networks have demonstrated their remarkable performance for feature extraction and pattern recognition in the last few years [2–5]. However, due to the contradiction between limited hardware resources and the requirement of high computational performance, it is still a challenge to implement large-scale deep neural networks for embedded real-time applications [6]. For example, research indicates that the unsupervised Deep Belief Network (DBN) shows the state-of-the-art accuracy for classifying hyperspectral remote sensing images [4]. However, it is technically impractical to deploy the DBN to process remote sensing images in real time, because the embedded systems carried by satellites or unmanned aerial vehicles are generally limited in memory space, computational resources, and power budget.

The fundamental computations of a feedforward DBN involve a large number of high-precision multiplications between the connection weights and the input data, which can be implemented using clusters of Central Processing Units (CPUs) or general-purpose Graphics Processing Units (GPUs) in powerful computers [7]. However, when memory and computational resources are limited in hardware, a more efficient algorithm would be ideal, designed for efficient hardware computing and only requiring simple fix-point computation and much fewer parameters, allowing larger networks to be implemented using System on Chips (SoCs) for real-time pattern recognition.

In this chapter, we present an algorithm-and-hardware codesign of the widely applied Deep Belief Network for embedded real-time image classification. For efficient hardware implementation, one important algorithmic consideration is the number of neural connections. The classic Deep Belief Network has fully connected neurons between adjacent layers (Fig. 7.1), resulting in high memory and computational complexity [8]. The second algorithmic consideration is data representation, which is an essential trade-off between accuracy and cost. Researches indicate that the Deep Belief

Deep Learning on Edge Computing Devices
https://doi.org/10.1016/B978-0-32-385783-3.00016-8

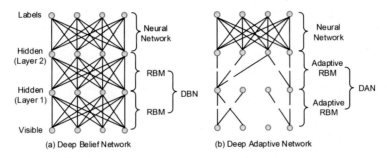

Figure 7.1 Typical deep neural networks implemented for pattern recognition applications. The neurons of the Deep Belief Network are fully connected between adjacent layers, whereas in a Deep Adaptive Network, the majority of neural connections (with zero weights) can be removed, and the reserved connections can be represented using single-bit integers, which is much more efficient for hardware implementation.

Networks trained with parameters of limited precision suffer from significant loss of accuracy [9–11]. To address these challenges, we propose an efficient training algorithm, named the Deep Adaptive Network (DAN), to explore the sparsity of neural connections. The DAN adaptively reduces the values of connection weights associated with negligible neurons to zeroes (Fig. 7.2) and robustly quantizes the small proportion of reserved connections using single-bit integers. A novel Sparse-Mapping-Memory (SMM) based architecture is designed to integrate the Deep Adaptive Network on Chip (DANoC). The characteristics of the DANoC coprocessor are summarized as follows.

- Memory efficient: The majority of the neural connections are removed by the DAN algorithm. Experiments show that over 80% of neural connections can be removed without degrading the classification accuracy. The reserved connection weights can be robustly quantized and represented using single-bit integers. Compared with the single-precision DBN, the proposed method can reduce the memory and computational resources by up to 99.9%.
- Power efficient: High memory efficiency enables the DANoC to reserve all the parameters on chip and reduces the power-hungry transfer operations between on-board memory and the DANoC coprocessor. Furthermore, the DANoC adopts an event-driven architecture, where the computation core is active only if the incoming visible unit is one.
- Computationally efficient: The single-bit representation allows the DANoC to replace the complicated high-precision multipliers with fast

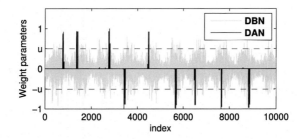

Figure 7.2 The connection weights of the DBN and DAN trained with the MNIST dataset. The DAN weights are sparse and separated as three groups, i.e., the zero, positive, and negative weights, leading to robust thresholding results and single-bit representation (±1).

area-efficient accumulators, which further relieve the computational bottleneck.

- Scalable and pipelined: The DANoC hardware is flexible and scalable in three ways. First, multiple layers of Sparse Neural Cores can be concatenated as a pipeline to form a multilayer deep neural network. Second, multiple pipelines are integrated in a chip for parallel acceleration. Third, the hardware implementation of the Sparse Neural Core is optimized and designed as a four-stage subpipeline for high-throughput applications.

With algorithm and hardware optimization, the DANoC could achieve the state-of-the-art performance of over 2000 effective giga-operations-per-second with less than 2 watts of power consumption.

Our method explores the sparsity of neural connections via a mixed norm-based regularization approach. It is a standard approach to achieve sparsity via the L_1 norm-based regularization. One famous example is the group lasso approach proposed by Yuan and Lin [12]. Our method can be seen as an extension of the group lasso for deep neural networks. Different from the group lasso, our work compresses the weight parameters using a mixed norm regularization, which allows us to control the tradeoff between rowwise and columnwise sparsity to achieve the highest compression rate.

Other attempts have been made to introduce sparsity into deep neural networks. Ranzato [13] proposed a deep encoder-decoder architecture to learn sparse representations. Lee [14] developed a variant of the Deep Belief Network to learn the sparse representations of the input images and found that the selected sparse features had some properties similar to visual area V2. Ji [15] proposed a sparse-response Deep Belief Network based on the rate-distortion theory, which attempted to encode the original data using as few bits as possible. Generally speaking, these researches focused on the sparsity of output activations; however, motivated by learning efficient architectures for hardware implementation, our work focused on exploring the sparsity of neural connections.

Previous researches have been attempted to incorporate ternary neural connections in traditional neural networks [16,17]. Very recently, there has been a growth of interest to compress the deep neural networks at algorithmic level for embedded applications. For example, Han [18] proposed a two-step training procedure to remove the small connection weights in the neural networks. Chen [19] used a hash function to group neural connections into different hash buckets according to different weight values. Han and Mao [20] proposed a three-step method to prune, quantize, and code the connection weights during the training process of the deep neural networks. Courbariaux [21] proposed a training process to learn the Deep Neural Networks with weights and activations constrained to +1 or −1. Rastegari [22] proposed a binary deep neural network, which quantized the weight parameters in each iteration of the training process. Generally speaking, these algorithms attempted to reduce the number of bits needed to represent the parameters, which yielded 1.2 to 49 times improvement in memory efficiency at the cost of degrading classification accuracy.

As a more efficient strategy, the DAN algorithm also allows the connections and activations to be represented using single-bit integers. Moreover, the DAN learns the optimal architecture of a sparse neural network, where the majority of neural connections are removed. Similar ideas have been recently demonstrated by Alvarez [23] and Pan [24], who proposed different regularization approaches to reduce the number of neuron connections in a deep network by up to 80% during training. Wen [25] proposed a Structured Sparsity Learning method, which learned a compact structure from a bigger deep neural network and reduced computational cost by 5.1 times. As the result of our two-step (regularize-and-quantize) strategy, the DAN hardware could achieve 160 to 640 times compression rate while still achieving competitively high accuracy comparing with the state-of-the-art approaches.

Thanks to the fast development of the deep learning approaches, the research of implementing dedicated hardware to accelerate neural network computation is booming. Himavathi and Byungik presented respective digital implementations using reconfigurable Field Programmable Gate Arrays (FPGAs) [6,8,26]. Sanni [27] presented an FPGA-based Deep Belief

Network using stochastic computation. Zhang et al. [28] quantitatively analyzed the Convolutional Neural Network (CNN) and implemented the quantized CNN using the FPGA device. Recently, Gokhale [29] implemented an FPGA-based coprocessor to accelerate deep neural networks for mobile applications. Performed independently from the algorithmic researches, these hardware designs generally adopted different quantization approaches for embedded implementation, which saved memory footprint but resulted in notable loss of classification accuracy. On the other hand, the proposed DANoC system was optimized from algorithm to hardware, which led to over three orders of magnitude of improvement in hardware efficiency without degrading classification accuracy.

7.2 Algorithm design and optimization

In this section, we present the proposed hardware-oriented unsupervised deep learning algorithm. As the background knowledge, we first introduce the training algorithm of the famous Deep Belief Network.

7.2.1 Deep belief network and restricted Boltzmann machine

A Deep Belief Network (DBN) is constructed by stacking multiple layers of Restricted Boltzmann Machines (RBMs) and using the output of the previous-layer RBM as the input of the next-layer RBM (Fig. 7.1). It is found that the higher-layer RBM tends to encode informative abstraction for classification. A standard RBM consists of two layers of units. First, a matrix $\mathbf{W} \in \mathbb{R}^{n \times d}$ is defined as the connection weights, where w_{ij} represents the connection between the visible unit v_i and the hidden unit h_j. Second, the parameters b_j and c_i are the biases for the hidden and visible units, respectively. Given the vector forms of the hidden units $\mathbf{h}$, the visible units $\mathbf{v}$, and the biases $\mathbf{b}$ and $\mathbf{c}$, the energy of a configuration $(\mathbf{v}, \mathbf{h})$ can be written as

$$E(\mathbf{v}, \mathbf{h}) = -\mathbf{b}^{\mathbf{T}}\mathbf{h} - \mathbf{c}^{\mathbf{T}}\mathbf{v} - \mathbf{v}^{\mathbf{T}}\mathbf{W}\mathbf{h}. \tag{7.1}$$

As in general Boltzmann machines, the probability distributions over the hidden and visible vectors are defined as

$$p(\mathbf{v}, \mathbf{h}) = \frac{1}{Z}e^{-E(\mathbf{v},\mathbf{h})}, \ \ Z = \sum_{\mathbf{v},\mathbf{h}} e^{-E(\mathbf{v},\mathbf{h})}. \tag{7.2}$$

Given Eq. (7.2), the marginal probability of the visible vector is

$$p(\mathbf{v}) = \frac{1}{Z}\sum_{\mathbf{h}} e^{-E(\mathbf{v},\mathbf{h})}. \qquad (7.3)$$

Since there are no direct connections between two hidden units at the same layer, the hidden units conditioned on $\mathbf{v}$ are independent of each other. Similarly, the visible units conditioned on $\mathbf{h}$ are also independent of each other. The units of a binary hidden layer, conditioned on the visible layer, are independent Bernoulli random variables. The binary state h_j of the jth hidden unit is set to 1 with probability

$$p(h_j = 1|\mathbf{v}) = \delta(\sum_i w_{ij}v_i + b_j), \qquad (7.4)$$

where $\delta(x) = 1/(1 + \exp(-x))$ is the sigmoid activation function. Similarly, if the visible units are binary, then the visible units, conditioned on the hidden layer, are also independent Bernoulli random variables. In this case, the binary state v_i of the ith visible unit is set to 1 with probability

$$p(v_i = 1|\mathbf{h}) = \delta(\sum_j w_{ij}h_j + c_i). \qquad (7.5)$$

On the other hand, if the visible units have real values, then the visible units, conditioned on the hidden layer, are independent Gaussian random variables defined as

$$p(v_i|\mathbf{h}) = \mathcal{G}(\sum_j w_{ij}h_j + c_i, 1), \qquad (7.6)$$

where $\mathcal{G}$ represents the Gaussian distribution. Suppose $\boldsymbol{\theta} = \{\mathbf{W}, \mathbf{b}, \mathbf{c}\}$ is the parameter set of the RBM. Since the RBM is a generative model, the parameters can be calculated by performing stochastic gradient descent on the log–likelihood of the training samples [30]. The probability that the network assigns to a sample $\mathbf{v}^{(k)}$ ($k = 1, \ldots, K$) is given by summing over all possible hidden vectors as

$$\arg\min_{\boldsymbol{\theta}} - \sum_k \log(\sum_{\mathbf{h}} e^{-E(\mathbf{v}^{(k)}, \mathbf{h}^{(k)})}). \qquad (7.7)$$

By solving Eq. (7.7) we can calculate the parameters offline and use them to configure the RBM. After training the RBM, the DBN can be built by stacking multiple layers of RBMs trained in a layer-by-layer manner.

7.2.2 Adaptive restricted Boltzmann machine

For efficient hardware implementation, a sparsely weighted variant of the RBM was proposed, named the Adaptive RBM (AdaRBM), which adds an extra regularization term in Eq. (7.7) to shrink the weights adaptively. The regularization term is based on a mixed matrix norm defined as

$$\|\mathbf{W}\|_M = \sum_i (\sum_j |w_{ij}|^2)^{1/2}, \tag{7.8}$$

where the indices i and j are treated differently. It is easy to prove that the mixed norm is a legitimate matrix norm, and it is different from the standard L_1 and L_2 matrix norms, i.e., $\|\mathbf{W}\|_{L_1} = \sum_i \sum_j |w_{ij}|$ and $\|\mathbf{W}\|_{L_2} = (\sum_i \sum_j w_{ij}^2)^{1/2}$.

The mixed matrix norm defined in Eq. (7.8) adds the vector norms of all rows in a matrix; therefore minimizing the mixed norm reduces the lengths of the matrix rows. It is worth noting that the shrinking process does not apply evenly to all rows. Shorter rows shrink faster than the rows with larger weights in the stochastic gradient descent process. As a result, the weights in short rows tend to shrink to zero after a finite number of iterations. Similarly, minimizing the mixed norm of a transposed matrix $\mathbf{W}^T$ can reduce the weights in shorter columns to zero. To achieve the maximum compression rate, the AdaRBM attempts to shrink the weight parameters in shorter rows and columns simultaneously by minimizing

$$\mathcal{R}_s(\mathbf{W}) = \lambda(\gamma \|\mathbf{W}\|_M + (1 - \gamma)\|\mathbf{W}^T\|_M), \tag{7.9}$$

where λ controls the sparsity of the weight parameters, and γ controls the balance between row sparsity and column sparsity. Formally, the AdaRBM training algorithm attempts to shrink the regularization term by incorporating it in the standard RBM of Eq. (7.7) as

$$\operatorname*{arg\,min}_{\boldsymbol{\theta}} - \sum_k \log(\sum_{\mathbf{h}} e^{-E(\mathbf{v}^{(k)}, \mathbf{h}^{(k)})})$$
$$+ \lambda(\gamma \|\mathbf{W}\|_M + (1 - \gamma)\|\mathbf{W}^T\|_M). \tag{7.10}$$

7.2.3 Training algorithm

The objective function of Eq. (7.10) is the sum of a log-likelihood term and a regularization term. The derivatives of the log probability and the

---

Algorithm 7.1: Training algorithm of the Adaptive RBM.

1: Given $\langle v_i h_j \rangle_{\text{model}}$ represents the distribution defined by running a Gibbs chain, the parameters can be updated using the contrastive divergence rule as

$$w_{ij} \Leftarrow w_{ij} + \epsilon(\langle v_i h_j \rangle_{\text{data}} - \langle v_i h_j \rangle_{\text{model}})$$

$$b_j \Leftarrow b_j + \epsilon(\langle h_j \rangle_{\text{data}} - \langle h_j \rangle_{\text{model}})$$

$$c_i \Leftarrow c_i + \epsilon(\langle v_i \rangle_{\text{data}} - \langle v_i \rangle_{\text{model}}),$$

where ϵ is a learning rate, and $\langle \cdot \rangle_{\text{model}}$ is the expectation over the reconstruction data;

2: Update w_{ij} using the gradient of $\mathcal{R}_s(\mathbf{W})$ as

$$w_{ij} \Leftarrow w_{ij} - \lambda(\gamma \frac{w_{ij}}{\alpha + \sqrt{\sum_i w_{ij}^2}} + (1 - \gamma) \frac{w_{ij}}{\alpha + \sqrt{\sum_j w_{ij}^2}}),$$

where α is a small constant to avoid zero denominator.

3: Check the constraint and repeat the update process until it achieves convergence.

---

regularization term with respect to the parameters can be expressed as

$$\frac{\partial \log p(\mathbf{v})}{\partial w_{ij}} = \langle v_i h_j \rangle_{\text{data}} - \langle v_i h_j \rangle_{\text{model}} + \frac{\partial \mathcal{R}_s(\mathbf{W})}{\partial w_{ij}}, \qquad (7.11)$$

$$\frac{\partial \log p(\mathbf{v})}{\partial b_j} = \langle h_j \rangle_{\text{data}} - \langle h_j \rangle_{\text{model}}, \qquad (7.12)$$

$$\frac{\partial \log p(\mathbf{v})}{\partial c_i} = \langle v_i \rangle_{\text{data}} - \langle v_i \rangle_{\text{model}}, \qquad (7.13)$$

$$\frac{\partial \mathcal{R}_s(\mathbf{W})}{\partial w_{ij}} = \lambda(\gamma \frac{w_{ij}}{\sqrt{\sum_i w_{ij}^2}} + (1 - \gamma) \frac{w_{ij}}{\sqrt{\sum_j w_{ij}^2}}), \qquad (7.14)$$

where $\langle \cdot \rangle_p$ indicates the expectation of the distribution p. Unfortunately, similarly to the RBM training process, the above equations are not tractable, because the computation of the expectations is very difficult; however, we can use the contrastive divergence (CD) with Gibbs sampling to approximate the optimal parameters in an iterative way [30]. On each iteration, we apply the contrastive divergence update rule, followed by one step of gradient descent of the regularization term as in Algorithm 7.1. According to Eq. (7.14), the shrinking process of the weight parameters is uneven. After a few hundred times of iterations, the weights in short rows and columns can be reduced to near zero, leading to sparse weight parameters. It is worth noting that the mix-norm regularization is not differentiable at point zero. In practice, a small constant, e.g., $\alpha = 0.01$, can be added in the denominator to improve the robustness of the training algorithm.

Similarly to the DBN, multiple layers of AdaRBMs can be stacked to compose a DAN, and the DAN can also be trained in a layer-by-layer style. Specifically, we can train the bottom AdaRBM with CD on the training data. With the parameters frozen and the hidden unit values inferred, these inferred values can be used as the input data to train the next layer of the network.

The Deep Adaptive Network, built with stacked AdaRBMs, is designed for efficient hardware implementation. Technically, the parameters of an AdaRBM are calculated offline with a four-step procedure and used to configure the DANoC hardware prototype. (1) The single-precision sparse parameters are calculated according to Algorithm 7.1; (2) The weight parameters are thresholded using a small positive value u, and the weights with small absolute values are removed; (3) The reserved positive and negative weights are represented as $+1$ and -1 respectively; (4) The activations are binarized using zero and one.

7.2.4 Properties of the deep adaptive network

The Deep Adaptive Network learns an efficient hardware-oriented network architecture featuring two properties.

- The neural connections of the DAN are sparse. The DAN adaptively reduces the connection weights associated with negligible visible units to zero, which can be removed for efficient hardware implementation.
- The activations of the DAN hidden units are sparse. Specifically, during the training phase, the AdaRBM uses $p(h_j = 1|\mathbf{v})$ as the jth output activation to the next layer. Since the short columns of the weight matrix are reduced to zero vectors, the output activations associated with zero columns become close to a constant $\delta(b_j)$ independent from the visible units. This property potentially makes the connection weights of the next-layer AdaRBM to be sparser.

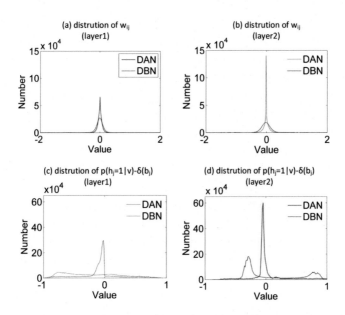

Figure 7.3 Empirical distributions of the connection weights and the activations of a two-layer DAN. Diagrams (a) and (b) show the distributions of w_{ij} for the first and second layers, respectively, (c) and (d) show the distributions of $p(h_j = 1|\mathbf{v})$ subtracted by the constant sigmoid (b_j). It is worth noting that for the DAN, the second-layer weights and activations seem sparser than the first layer.

Fig. 7.3 illustrates these two properties. Two deep neural networks of the same configuration (784–800–800) are built to select the features from the MNIST dataset. It seems that most DAN weights are close to zero, which are much sparser than the DBN weights. Meanwhile, by subtracting the constant vector $\delta(\mathbf{b})$ the output activations of the AdaRBMs become notably sparser than the standard RBM (Fig. 7.3(c,d)). It is worth noting that, as shown in Fig. 7.3(b), the weight parameters become sparser in the second layer than in the first layer. It seems that the sparse activations of the first layer make the second–layer connection weights sparser.

7.3 Near-memory computing architecture

The DANoC system is an efficient, high–throughput, and scalable hardware prototype of the Deep Adaptive Network built using off-the-shelf FPGA devices. The basic building block of the hardware is a Sparse Neural Core (SNC) featuring an efficient Sparse-Mapping-Memory (SMM) based architecture. Fig. 7.4 shows an example of the cross-bar SMM designed to

Visible unit	Length	Start Address
1	0	-
2	1	0x00
3	0	-
4	2	0x01
5	0	-
6	0	-
7	0	-
8	1	0x03
9	1	0x04
Events	Address mapping table	

	Hidden unit	Weight	Group Size
0x00	c	-1	2
0x01	c	1	1
	g	1	3
0x03	d	-1	4
0x04	h	1	1
	Weight table		

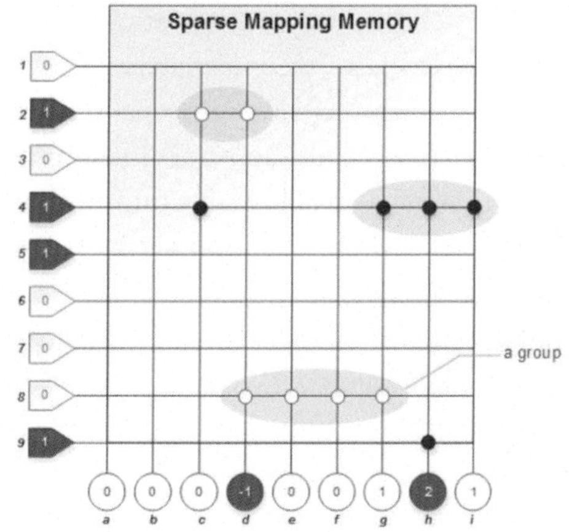

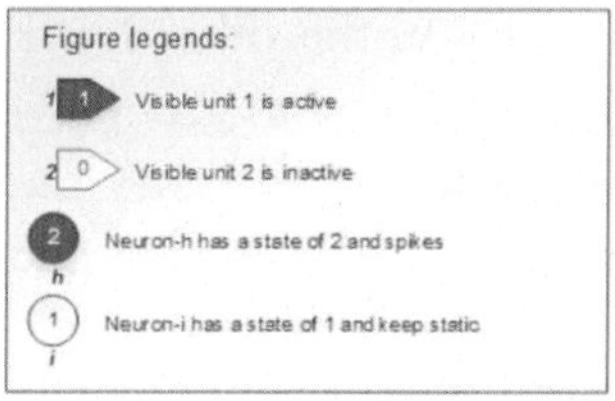

Sparse Mapping Memory

Figure legends:
1 → Visible unit 1 is active
2 → Visible unit 2 is inactive
2 / h → Neuron-h has a state of 2 and spikes
1 / i → Neuron-i has a state of 1 and keep static

a group

Figure 7.4 The sparse mapping memory (SMM) in the Sparse Neural Core. Each SMM consists of two tables to maintain the group addresses and the nonzero weight groups.

implement a sparsely connected AdaRBM with nine visible units and nine hidden units. Each cross point in the SMM represents a connection weight w_{ij} between the ith visible unit (left) and the jth hidden unit (down). In a functional point of view, the input data of each core are processed as coded address events. The address event i is active when the ith visible unit is one, which triggers a look-up operation; otherwise, the address event i is inactive, and the core will check the next visible unit for an active address event. No look-up operation will be fired until a nonzero visible unit is found. The zeros in the input data stream are omitted, and only the spikes of ones can activate the core.

The look-up operation of the ith address event has three steps. First, the incoming event activates the Address Mapping Table, which reads out the starting address i and the length of the weight group. If the ith visible unit is connected to zero hidden units, then the core goes on to check the next visible unit. Secondly, the binary weights of all hidden units connected with the visible unit i are read out from the Weight Table. Then each hidden unit updates the state value s_j in the Neural State Table by w_{ij}. When the neural state exceeds its threshold b_j, the neuron produces a spike, and its neural state is reset to 0; this spike is then encoded and sent off as an address event to the next Sparse Neural Core. The binary representation allows the DANoC to use power-efficient threshold operations to implement the sigmoid activation function.

The weight-decay optimization of the AdaRBM leads to rowwise and columnwise sparse weight matrix. The hardware design of the SNC takes advantage of the two-dimensional sparsity to improve hardware efficiency. Since the SNC only activates look-up operations when connections associated with a given visible unit exist, the rowwise sparsity allows the DANoC to save time and power by overlooking the majority of the visible units whose associated connections are all removed. On the other hand, the columnwise sparsity makes the nonzero weights in a row to group together. Therefore the Weight Table of the Sparse Mapping Memory can reduce memory consumption and computational time by preserving and reading weights in groups.

A block diagram of the DANoC coprocessor is shown in Fig. 7.5. The system on chip has three main components: two host ARM Cortex A9 processors, a coprocessor, and an external memory controller. The coprocessor comprises an array of pipelined Sparse Neural Cores and a control module. Multiple pipelines of deep neural networks can be implemented in parallel in the DANoC. Each pipeline contains multiple cascaded Sparse Neural Cores, and each core can be configured as an AdaRBM layer or a classifier layer. The DANoC uses respective on-chip block RAMs to implement the Address Mapping Table, the Weight Table, the Neural State Table, and the Threshold Table. The accesses of these block RAMs are coordinated as a four-stage subpipeline to maximize the throughput.

The memory complexity of the DANoC chip is mainly determined by the size of the Weight Table, which is proportional to $n \times d \times \sigma \times \log(s)/s$, where $n \times d$ is the size of the weight matrix, σ is the ratio of reserved connections, and s is the average size a weight group. In practice, the DANoC can save 99.3% to 99.9% weight memory compared with the standard single-precision DBN. The binary representation achieved by the DAN algorithm enables the DANoC to substitute the complicated floating-point multipliers for power-efficient accumulators. Moreover, since the latency of a binary accumulator is significantly lower than a floating-point multi-

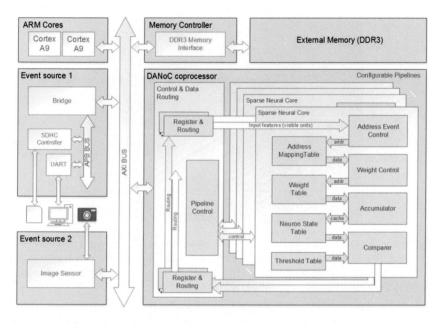

Figure 7.5 Block diagram of the DAN on chip (DANoC), which consists of two host processors, a coprocessor and an external memory controller. The coprocessor consists of an array of pipelined deep neural networks, and each pipeline is composed of multiple Sparse Neural Cores. Each core can be configured as an AdaRBM or a neural network classifier.

plier, the DANoC can process the input remote sensing and video images in real time without jamming the pipeline.

The DANoC prototype is implemented using the Xilinx Zynq FPGA device, which is a programmable System on Chip (SoC) (Fig. 7.6). The ARM host processors work at 800 MHz and the coprocessor works at 100 MHz in the SoC. The Zynq7Z020 FPGA has 4.9 Mb on-chip block RAM. The hardware prototype contains 1 GB 533 MHz DDR3 on-board memory and 3.8 GB/s full-duplex memory bandwidth. The peak power consumption of the entire board is 8 watts, and the power consumption is less than 2 watts for the FPGA device. The Zynq platform is chosen because its performance increases linearly as the number of pipelines increases. To evaluate the scalability of the DANoC, a high-end version of the DANoC coprocessor is implemented using the Xilinx Zynq7100 FPGA, which contains 26.5 Mb on-chip block RAM and allows us to fit up to 30 pipelines in a single chip.

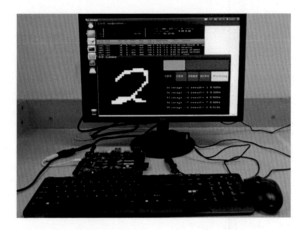

Figure 7.6 The DANoC hardware prototype applied for classifying images of handwritten digits. The classification of each image contains 1.28 million operations, the DANoC can process one image in less than 0.24 ms, and the low-price Zynq7Z020-based DANoC achieves effective 319 GOPS at 495 mw.

The host ARM processors are responsible for parsing a deep network and controlling the transfer of input and configuration data to the coprocessor. The coprocessor is implemented on programmable logic and interfaces with the host processors via the AXI bus. Input data are encoded as address events and streamed into the coprocessor, one data word per clock cycle. Data words are organized as an array, with data words streamed in one row at a time. These data words can be pixels in case of images or videos. The DDR memory controller interfaces the pipelines with external memory. Its purpose is to route independent data streams and feed data to the DANoC pipelines. The router is implemented as a crossbar switch, allowing the coprocessor to access multiple memory buffers at once with full-duplex data transactions.

7.4 Applications of deep adaptive network on chip

In this section, we evaluate the DAN algorithm and the DANoC hardware prototype using three different applications, i.e., recognizing images of handwritten digits, classifying hyperspectral remote sensing images, and an application of video-based self-driving toy robot car.

7.4.1 Experiment setting and measurements

We implement the sparsely connected DAN with binary connections and activations in four steps. In each step, the feedforward neural network becomes more efficient. To distinguish these networks, we list the DANs with different precisions:

- DAN: single-precision DAN;
- DAN_t: single-precision DAN whose majority of connections associated with zero weights are removed;
- DAN_b: fix-point DAN with binary connection weights;
- DAN_B: fix-point DAN with binary connection weights and binary activations.

To evaluate the sparsity of neural connections, we use the ratio of reserved weights σ as the sparsity measurement, which is controlled by the threshold value u as

$$\sigma = 1 - \frac{\mathcal{N}(u)}{\text{total number of weights}} \times 100\%, \qquad (7.15)$$

where $\mathcal{N}(u)$ indicates the number of weights whose absolute values are smaller than u. Specifically, the sparsity measurement $\sigma \in [0, 1]$ reaches 0 if $u = \max_{ij} |w_{ij}|$. The σ measurement is an important tradeoff between efficiency and classification accuracy, and a typical range of σ is 5%–25% for the examined datasets.

7.4.2 MNIST handwritten images

MNIST is a benchmark image classification dataset [31]. It consists of a training set of 60000 and a test set of 10000 28 × 28 gray-scale images representing digits ranging from 0 to 9 (Fig. 7.7). Two networks, a DAN (784-800-800-10) and a DBN (784-800-800-10), are built to extract features from the images in the MNIST dataset. We use the training set of 60000 images to simultaneously fit the DAN and DBN. The parameters of the DAN are then thresholded and binarized. Respective neural network classifiers are connected with the DAN and DBN. The experiment shows that the DAN_t with only 25% connections reserved has almost the same classification accuracy (98.83%) as the original DBN (98.84%) with full connections.

Fig. 7.7 illustrates the DAN_b with binary connection weights. The weight parameters are shown in subgraph (b). The inferred values are shown in subgraph (a). As a result of the mixed-norm weight-decay and

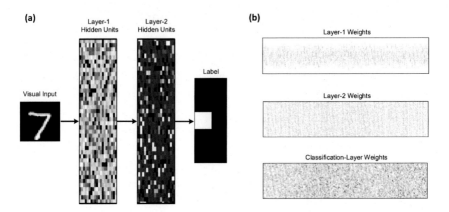

Figure 7.7 The sparsely connected binary-weighted Deep Adaptive Network (DAN$_b$) learned from the MNIST dataset. A neural network classifier is connected to the Deep Adaptive Network for recognizing the label (0–9) of a given image.

threshold process, the weight matrices of the first-layer and the second-layer AdaRBMs become very sparse, and the nonzero weights tend to cluster into different groups.

We change the parameter λ from 10^{-1} to 10^{-8} to evaluate its relation to classification accuracy. Our experiment randomly selects 10000 images for training, and tests the DAN, the DBN, the DBN with L_1-norm weight-decay (DBN$_1$), and the DBN with L_2-norm weight-decay (DBN$_2$) over the rest images. The experiment is carried out ten times, and the average accuracies are shown in Fig. 7.8(a). It seems that the DAN, DBN, and DBN$_2$ have similar classification accuracy when λ is smaller than 10^{-4}; however, the DBN$_1$ has noticeably lower accuracy.

Since the parameter λ controls the sparsity of the weight parameters in a Deep Adaptive Network, it can affect the efficiency of hardware implementation. Fig. 7.8(b) shows the relation between the ratio of reserved weights σ and the value of λ. A typical threshold value $u = 0.1$ and $\gamma = 0.5$ are set. Results show that the ratio of reserved weights drops significantly from about 50% to less than 5% when λ changes from 10^{-8} to 10^{-1}. Experiment also shows that the second layer of the DAN is over 15% sparser than the first layer.

We performed a experiment to illustrate how the parameter γ controls the tradeoff between rowwise sparsity and columnwise sparsity of the weight matrix. The weights of the DAN$_t$ with different values of γ are examined. We compare the rowwise matrix norm $\|\mathbf{W}\|_M$ and the columnwise

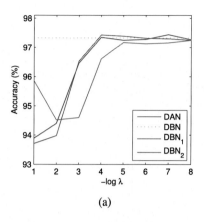 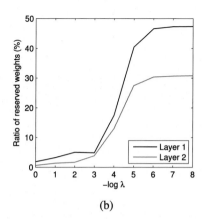

(a)   (b)

Figure 7.8 (a) The classification accuracies of the DBNs and the DAN change as λ changes from 10^{-1} to 10^{-8} ($\gamma = 0.5$). The DBN$_1$ and DBN$_2$ are single-precision DBNs with L$_1$ and L$_2$ norm weight decays, respectively. (b) The ratio of reserved weights ($\sigma\%$) of each layer in the DAN is controlled by the parameter λ ($u = 0.1$, $\gamma = 0.5$).

matrix norm $\|\mathbf{W}^T\|_M$ and have two observations. First, $\|\mathbf{W}^T\|_M$ increases as γ increases, whereas $\|\mathbf{W}\|_M$ drops as γ increases. This observation is coherent with the optimization formulation of Eq. (7.10). Second, the weight matrix of the second-layer AdaRBM has about 20% smaller mixed norm than the first-layer AdaRBM. This observation indicates that the second-layer weights may be sparser than the first-layer weights, which is coherent with the results of Fig. 7.8(b).

Fig. 7.9(a) compares the accuracy of the classic neural network classifiers proceeded by the DBN and DANs of different precisions. To compare the influence of quantization on the examined approaches, the weights of the DBNs are thresholded and quantized with the same setting as the DAN. Experiment shows that, generally speaking, the DAN is sparse and robust with the binary quantization operation. When the ratio of reserved weights σ changes from 0% to 5%, the classification accuracy of the DAN$_b$ quickly climbs to over 90%. However, the classification accuracies of the DBN (54.2%), DBN$_1$ (19.2%), and DBN$_2$ (67.4%) show much worse results with 5% connections reserved. It seems that the DAN$_b$ shows almost no drop in classification accuracy when more than 10% connections are reserved. Moreover, the deviation results indicate that the DBN$_1$, DBN$_2$, and DAN are all relatively stabler than the original DBN when the ratio of reserved weights decreases. The deviation of the DAN quickly shrinks when more than 15% weights are reserved.

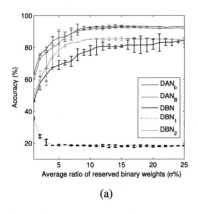
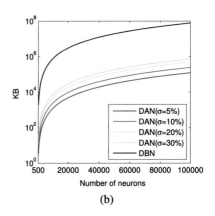

(a)   (b)

Figure 7.9 (a) Classification accuracy of the DANs and DBNs with different weight decay approaches. The connection weights are thresholded with the σ% significant weights reserved and represented using single-bit integers. (b) Memory required for weight parameters of the DBN and DAN.

To achieve higher hardware efficiency, the DAN can use binary activations and binary weights. Fig. 7.9(a) also shows the influence of adopting binary activation on classification accuracy. The activations of the DAN_B are thresholded and binarized using a constant 0.5. As shown in Fig. 7.9(a), the accuracy of the neural network classifier proceeded by the DAN_B is significantly higher than the DBN. By adopting binary weights and activations the DANoC coprocessor can replace the complex floating-point multipliers with simple fix-point accumulators and implements the sigmoid activation function using simple threshold operations.

By adopting the sparse binary connections the DAN becomes 99.3% ($\sigma = 20$%) to 99.9% ($\sigma = 5$%) more memory efficient than the single-precision DBN. Fig. 7.9(b) shows the theoretical results of the memory used by the DAN and original DBN. The memory complexity of the deep neural networks increases as the number of neurons increases. The present DBNs are usually implemented using 32-bit representation; however, with sparse and binary weights, the DAN_b can improve the memory efficiency by two to three orders of magnitude.

7.4.3 Hyperspectral remote sensing images

The second experiment applies the DAN algorithm and the DANoC system to the hyperspectral remote sensing application. Differently from visible-light images, the hyperspectral images contain information from across the electromagnetic spectrum. Fig. 7.10 shows the Pavia Center

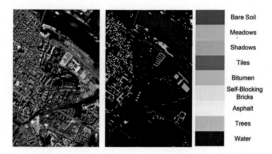

Bare Soil

Meadows

Shadows

Tiles

Bitumen

Self-Blocking
Bricks

Asphalt

Trees

Water

Figure 7.10 The Pavia Center image and the ground-truth labels for each pixel. The Pavia Center set has 1.2 million samples. The DBN-based classification of each sample contains 10.9 million operations, and the Zynq7100-based DANoC achieves 2036 effective GOPS at 1.9 watts power consumption.

Table 7.1 Examined hyperspectral datasets.

Datasets	Bands	Samples (million)	Features	Classes
Indian Pines	224	0.02	2016	16
Salinas	224	0.11	2016	16
Pavia University	103	0.37	927	9
Pavia Center	102	1.20	918	9

dataset, which contains 1.2 million samples. Each pixel in the image is recorded with 102 spectral bands covering the wavelengths from 401 nm to 889 nm. The goal of classification is determining nine labels associated with each pixel.

Our experiments examine four well-known datasets of hyperspectral images (Table 7.1). All the examined datasets are downloaded from the hyperspectral website [32]. The scene of the India Pines is gathered by the AVIRIS sensor and consists of 21025 samples with 224 spectral reflectance bands in the wavelength ranging from 0.4×10^{-6} to 2.5×10^{-6} meters. The label of each pixel falls into sixteen classes. The Salinas dataset is collected by the 224-band AVIRIS sensor over the Salinas Valley, California, and is characterized by high spatial resolution (3.7-meter pixels). The area covered comprises 11.11 thousand samples of 16 classes. Similar to the Pavia Center data set, the Pavia University set has nine classes and 0.37 million samples recorded with 103 spectral bands.

Differently from traditional technologies, the hyperspectral imaging can get the spatial and spectral data simultaneously, resulting in high-dimensional samples. For practical remote sensing applications, the number of labeled training samples for each class is usually less than a few hundreds.

Table 7.2 The latest researches of hyperspectral image classification.

Author	Approaches	Salinas	Indian Pines	Pavia University
Zhou	DANoC hardware[a]	94.19	89.03	95.33
Yue [33]	CNN regression	–	–	95.18
Yuan [34]	CART kNN	89.00	81.00	89.00
Wang [35]	sparse coding	–	93.11	90.41
Kuo [36]	kernel SVM	–	88.70	94.00
Ramzi [37]	adaboost SVM	93.12	91.59	94.28
Li [38]	Markov random filed	–	–	94.96
Plaza [39]	multinomial regression	–	76.71	76.03
Li [40]	Tikhonov method	–	89.00	92.00
Chen [41]	Autoencoder	–	–	98.52
Liu [42]	Autoencoder	95.50	–	96.40
Zhao [43]	BLDE+CNN	–	–	96.98

[a] The DANoC hardware implements the DAN with binary connections and activations. The compared approaches are generally implemented using 32-bit floating-point representation.

The scarcity of labeled training samples can cause a significant drop in classification accuracy for supervised approaches, which is known as the Hughes phenomenon. Therefore an *unsupervised* feature extraction process is usually applied before hyperspectral classification. Recently, there has been a lot interest in the remote sensing area to apply the deep learning algorithms for hyperspectral classification, and the DBN has been reported as the state-of-the-art for extracting features from hyperspectral images [4]. However, it is usually a challenge to deploy the DBN to process remote sensing images in real time, because the embedded systems carried by satellites or unmanned aerial vehicles are generally limited in hardware resources. In this experiment, we show that the efficient DAN algorithm and the DANoC system can provide competitive results with the state-of-the-art approaches for classifying hyperspectral images (Table 7.2).

Fig. 7.11 shows our DAN-based classification process of the spatial–spectral samples, which consists of four steps: (1) Normalization and whitening are applied to reduce the correlation between features; (2) The neighbor region of the target pixel is selected (red square), and the spatial–spectral sample is flattened and arranged as a vector; (3) A DAN is trained and built to extract the features from the high-dimensional vector; (4) The extracted features are classified using a neural network classifier.

Given a target pixel, a neighbor region of nine pixels is constructed to form a high-dimensional spatial–spectral sample. Different deep neural net-

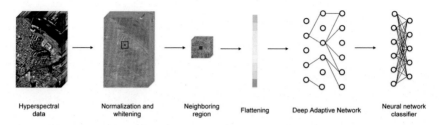

Figure 7.11 Spatial–spectral classification of the hyperspectral data using the proposed Deep Adaptive Network. Each pixel in the hyperspectral data is recorded with 102 spectral bands covering the wavelengths from 401 nm to 889 nm.

works are trained over the Indian Pines dataset (1800-2000-2000), the Salinas dataset (1836-2000-2000), the Pavia Center dataset (918-1000-1000), and the Pavia University dataset (927-1000-1000) for feature selection. Our experiment compares the proposed method with the Deep Belief Network (DBN), the Principal Component Analysis (PCA), and the Independent Component Analysis (ICA), all of which have been proven to be effective for processing the hyperspectral data. Different classifiers, including the Neural Network classifier (NN), the Logistic Regression classifier (LR), the Support Vector Machine (SVM), the Naive Bayes (NB), and the Decision Tree (DT), are examined. All the compared classifiers are implemented using the WEKA software [44]. To calculate the classification accuracy, we randomly selected 50% of unlabeled hyperspectral samples for training the unsupervised DAN, the PCA, and the ICA, and used the remaining samples for testing. The classifiers are trained with 25% labels randomly selected from the training set. The experiment was repeated ten times, and the average classification accuracy and derivation were calculated. Experiment results in Table 7.3 show that the DAN algorithm achieves the highest classification accuracy among all compared approaches over three of the examined datasets (90.90% to 99.59%).

Table 7.2 compares the binary DAN implemented in the DANoC system with the optimal results reported by the latest hyperspectral researches [33–40]. All these researches use the same spatial–spectral samples and similar experiment settings. It seems that the DANoC system can achieve competitive results with the-state-of-the-art approaches by taking the advantage of the large-volume unlabeled samples. It is worth noting that the DAN even outperforms some deep learning based approaches including the CNN. Since the labeled training samples are limited and expensive for

Table 7.3 Standard hyperspectral classification approaches.

Methods	Indian Pines	Salinas	Pavia Center	Pavia University
DAN + neural network	**90.90** ±0.06	*95.52* ±0.03	**99.59** ±0.23	**96.72** ±0.12
DBN + neural network	*90.31* ±0.17	**96.02** ±0.13	*99.50* ±0.13	*95.89* ±0.08
PCA + linear regression	66.76 ±0.16	93.14 ±0.07	99.13 ±0.03	93.48 ±0.07
PCA + naive Bayes	62.11 ±0.21	90.35 ±0.10	96.06 ±0.09	83.2 ±0.13
PCA + decision tree	68.18 ±0.16	89.32 ±0.08	97.57 ±0.05	88.78 ±0.02
PCA + SVM	68.77 ±0.23	93.35 ±0.22	99.16 ±0.05	93.3 ±0.15
ICA + linear regression	68.26 ±0.16	93.51 ±0.07	99.32 ±0.03	93.69 ±0.07
ICA + naive Bayes	66.41 ±0.21	93.44 ±0.10	99.38 ±0.07	85.94 ±0.09
ICA + decision tree	59.71 ±0.18	90.47 ±0.09	96.02 ±0.05	87.87 ±0.13
ICA + SVM	68.26 ±0.22	93.51 ±0.22	99.32 ±0.28	93.3 ±0.21

remote sensing applications, the lack of labeled training data degrades the performance of supervised approaches.

With algorithm-level and hardware-level optimization, the DANoC coprocessor achieves competitive performance with the state-of-the-art hardware implementations [27–29,45]. In our hardware experiments, the performance of the DANoC system is estimated using the number of multiplications required in a standard Deep Belief Network. Two versions of DANoC systems are implemented using the Zynq7Z020 and Zynq7100 FPGA devices. As shown in Table 7.4, the low-cost Zynq7Z020 DANoC achieves high performance of 615 to 841 giga-operations-per-second-per-watt, which allows the DANoC chip to process 31.2 to 53.9 thousand hyperspectral samples per second. The peak performance achieved by the Zynq7100 DANoC chip is 2077 effective giga-operations-per-second, which is the state-of-the-art among the latest FPGA-based hardware implementations (Table 7.5). The high performance is achieved at less than 2

Table 7.4 Performance of the DANoC hardware prototype.

Data sets	Zynq7Z020 @ 410–495 mw				Zynq7100 @ 1760–1930 mw			
	Number of pipelines	Throughput (thousand samples per second)	Effective performance (GOPS/watt)	Single chip performance (GOPS)	Number of pipelines	Throughput (thousand samples per second)	Effective performance (GOPS/watt)	Single chip performance (GOPS)
MNIST	5	60.1	774	381	25	300.5	992	1903
Indian Pines	1	31.2	615	237	5	156.0	714	1185
Salinas	1	31.2	615	238	5	156.0	714	1189
Pavia Center	4	53.8	833	407	20	215.2	1073	2036
Pavia University	4	53.9	841	415	20	215.6	1079	2077
Robot Car (sign/road)	3/3	52.5/75.2	677	319	15/15	262.5/376.0	879	1593

Table 7.5 Peak performance of the latest hardware deep neural network accelerators.

Author	Type	Platform	Speed (GOPS)	Power (mw)	Precision
This work	FPGA	Zynq7Z020	415	495	fix 1
	FPGA	Zynq7100	2077	1930	fix 1
Sanmi [27]	FPGA	Kintex7350	–	–	fix12
Zhang [28]	FPGA	Virtex7	612	18610	fix32
Gokhale [29]	FPGA	Zynq7Z045	227	4000	fix16
Li [45]	FPGA	StratixV	410	1114	fix 16
Du [46]	layout	65 nm	194	320	fix16
Pham [47]	layout	45 nm SOI	320	600	fix1
Cavigelli [48]	silicon	65 nm	196	510	fix12
Andri [49]	silicon	65 nm	423	153	fix1

watts of chip-level power consumption, which is orders of magnitude more efficient than CPU- and GPU-based solutions.

7.4.4 Real-time analysis of video images

Besides the remote sensing applications, which are our primary motivation, we also evaluate the DANoC hardware for real-time video processing. In this experiment a DANoC hardware prototype is mounted on a toy robot car for automatic driving (Fig. 7.12). The robot car has two 640-480 video cameras connected with the hardware board via respective USB ports. One camera is used to track the road, and the other is used to recognize 12 traffic signs. The video streams are captured and thresholded as binary frames using software running on the ARM host processors. Then the image frames are split as 16-16 (road) and 32-32 (traffic sign) windows with 8-pixel step size, and the images are arranged as binary streams and routed to the DANoC coprocessor for feature extraction and classification. The classification results are then sent back to the host processor to automatically control the toy robot car.

Two types of DAN pipelines are implemented in the DANoC coprocessor for recognizing the traffic signs and the road. Each pipeline uses two Sparse Neural Cores to implement a stacked DAN and one core to implement the neural network classifier. Eight video clips recoded with different light conditions and camera angles are used to train and test the DAN algorithm offline. An experiment shows that the DANoC coprocessor achieves 98.2% correct rate for recognizing 12 traffic signs and 98.9% correct rate for recognizing the road. The performance of the DANoC system is estimated

Figure 7.12 A self-driving robot car equipped with a DANoC hardware prototype. The robot car has two cameras; one is used to track the road (left), and the other is used to recognize the traffic signs (right). Two types of deep neural networks are integrated in the DANoC, which achieve 98.2% correct rate for recognizing 12 traffic signs and 98.9% correct rate for recognizing the road. The Zynq7100-based DANoC coprocessor achieves the state-of-the-art peak performance of 1593 GOPS and is able to process 67 frames of 640-480 video in real time.

using the number of multiplications required in a standard Deep Belief Network of the same configuration. The Zynq7Z020 DANoC with six pipelines of deep neural networks achieves 319 giga–operations–per–second with 478-mw power consumption. The high-performance Zynq7100-based DANoC could integrate up to 30 pipelines in single FPGA chip, which enables it to process 67 frames in real-time with the peak performance of 1593 effective giga–operations–per–second.

References

[1] X. Zhou, S. Li, F. Tang, S. Hu, Z. Lin, L. Zhang, DaNoC: An efficient algorithm and hardware codesign of deep neural networks on chip, IEEE Transactions on Neural Networks and Learning Systems 29 (7) (2017) 3176–3187.

[2] G. Hinton, L. Deng, D. Yu, G.E. Dahl, A.-r. Mohamed, N. Jaitly, A. Senior, V. Vanhoucke, P. Nguyen, T.N. Sainath, et al., Deep neural networks for acoustic modeling in speech recognition: The shared views of four research groups, IEEE Signal Processing Magazine 29 (6) (2012) 82–97.

[3] G.E. Hinton, R.R. Salakhutdinov, Reducing the dimensionality of data with neural networks, Science 313 (5786) (2006) 504–507.

[4] Y. Chen, X. Zhao, X. Jia, Spectral–spatial classification of hyperspectral data based on deep belief network, IEEE Journal of Selected Topics in Applied Earth Observations and Remote Sensing 8 (6) (2015) 2381–2392.

[5] O. Vinyals, S.V. Ravuri, Comparing multilayer perceptron to deep belief network tandem features for robust ASR, in: Proceedings of IEEE International Conference on Acoustics, Speech and Signal Processing, 2011, pp. 4596–4599.

[6] L.P. Maguire, T.M. McGinnity, B. Glackin, A. Ghani, A. Belatreche, J. Harkin, Challenges for large-scale implementations of spiking neural networks on FPGAs, Neurocomputing 71 (1–3) (2007) 13–29.

[7] N. Lopes, B. Ribeiro, An evaluation of multiple feed-forward networks on GPUs, International Journal of Neural Systems 21 (01) (2011) 31–47.

[8] S. Himavathi, D. Anitha, A. Muthuramalingam, Feedforward neural network implementation in FPGA using layer multiplexing for effective resource utilization, IEEE Transactions on Neural Networks 18 (3) (2007) 880–888.

[9] S. Draghici, On the capabilities of neural networks using limited precision weights, Neural Networks 15 (3) (2002) 395–414.

[10] J.L. Holi, J.-N. Hwang, Finite precision error analysis of neural network hardware implementations, IEEE Transactions on Computers 42 (3) (1993) 281–290.

[11] S. Gupta, A. Agrawal, K. Gopalakrishnan, P. Narayanan, Deep learning with limited numerical precision, in: Proceedings of International Conference on Machine Learning, 2015, pp. 1737–1746.

[12] M. Yuan, Y. Lin, Model selection and estimation in regression with grouped variables, Journal of the Royal Statistical Society: Series B (Statistical Methodology) 68 (1) (2006) 49–67.

[13] M. Ranzato, Y.-L. Boureau, Y. LeCun, et al., Sparse feature learning for deep belief networks, Advances in Neural Information Processing Systems 20 (2007) 1185–1192.

[14] H. Lee, C. Ekanadham, A. Ng, Sparse deep belief net model for visual area V2, in: Proceedings of International Conference on Neural Information Processing Systems, vol. 20, 2007, pp. 873–880.

[15] N.-N. Ji, J.-S. Zhang, C.-X. Zhang, A sparse-response deep belief network based on rate distortion theory, Pattern Recognition 47 (9) (2014) 3179–3191.

[16] S. Abramson, D. Saad, E. Marom, Training a network with ternary weights using the CHIR algorithm, IEEE Transactions on Neural Networks 4 (6) (1993) 997–1000.

[17] F. Aviolat, E. Mayoraz, A constructive training algorithm for feedforward neural networks with ternary weights, in: Proceedings of European Symposium on Artificial Neural Networks, vol. 94, 1994, pp. 123–128.

[18] S. Han, J. Pool, J. Tran, W.J. Dally, Learning both weights and connections for efficient neural networks, in: Proceedings of International Conference on Neural Information Processing Systems, vol. 1, 2015, pp. 1135–1143.

[19] W. Chen, J. Wilson, S. Tyree, K. Weinberger, Y. Chen, Compressing neural networks with the hashing trick, in: Proceedings of International Conference on Machine Learning, 2015, pp. 2285–2294.

[20] S. Han, H. Mao, W.J. Dally, Deep compression: Compressing deep neural networks with pruning, trained quantization and Huffman coding, arXiv:1510.00149 [abs].

[21] M. Courbariaux, I. Hubara, D. Soudry, R. El-Yaniv, Y. Bengio, Binarized neural networks: Training deep neural networks with weights and activations constrained to +1 or −1, arXiv:1602.02830 [abs].

[22] M. Rastegari, V. Ordonez, J. Redmon, A. Farhadi, XNOR-Net: ImageNet classification using binary convolutional neural networks, in: Proceedings of European Conference on Computer Vision, 2016, pp. 525–542.

[23] J.M. Alvarez, M. Salzmann, Learning the number of neurons in deep networks, in: Proceedings of International Conference on Neural Information Processing Systems, 2016, pp. 2270–2278.

[24] W. Pan, H. Dong, Y. Guo, DropNeuron: Simplifying the structure of deep neural networks, arXiv:1606.07326 [abs].

[25] W. Wen, C. Wu, Y. Wang, Y. Chen, H. Li, Learning structured sparsity in deep neural networks, in: Proceedings of International Conference on Neural Information Processing Systems, 2016, pp. 2082–2090.

[26] B. Ahn, Computation of deep belief networks using special-purpose hardware architecture, in: Proceeding of the International Joint Conference on Neural Networks, 2014, pp. 141–148.

[27] K. Sanni, G. Garreau, J.L. Molin, A.G. Andreou, FPGA implementation of a deep belief network architecture for character recognition using stochastic computation, in: Proceedings of Annual Conference on Information Sciences and Systems, 2015, pp. 1–5.

[28] C. Zhang, P. Li, G. Sun, Y. Guan, B. Xiao, J. Cong, Optimizing FPGA-based accelerator design for deep convolutional neural networks, in: Proceedings of ACM/SIGDA International Symposium on Field-Programmable Gate Arrays, 2015, pp. 161–170.

[29] V. Gokhale, J. Jin, A. Dundar, B. Martini, E. Culurciello, A 240 G-ops/s mobile coprocessor for deep neural networks, in: Proceedings of IEEE Conference on Computer Vision and Pattern Recognition, 2014, pp. 682–687.

[30] G.E. Hinton, A practical guide to training restricted Boltzmann machines, in: Neural Networks: Tricks of the Trade, 2012, pp. 599–619.

[31] Y. LeCun, L. Bottou, Y. Bengio, P. Haffner, Gradient-based learning applied to document recognition, Proceedings of the IEEE 86 (11) (1998) 2278–2324.

[32] ECU hyperspectral website, URL http://www.ehu.eus/ccwintco/index.php?title= Hyperspectral_Remote_Sensing_Scenes#Pavia_Centre_scene.

[33] J. Yue, W. Zhao, S. Mao, H. Liu, Spectral–spatial classification of hyperspectral images using deep convolutional neural networks, Remote Sensing Letters 6 (6) (2015) 468–477.

[34] Y. Yuan, G. Zhu, Q. Wang, Hyperspectral band selection by multitask sparsity pursuit, IEEE Transactions on Geoscience and Remote Sensing 53 (2) (2014) 631–644.

[35] Z. Wang, N.M. Nasrabadi, T.S. Huang, Semisupervised hyperspectral classification using task-driven dictionary learning with Laplacian regularization, IEEE Transactions on Geoscience and Remote Sensing 53 (3) (2014) 1161–1173.

[36] B.-C. Kuo, H.-H. Ho, C.-H. Li, C.-C. Hung, J.-S. Taur, A kernel-based feature selection method for SVM with RBF kernel for hyperspectral image classification, IEEE Journal of Selected Topics in Applied Earth Observations and Remote Sensing 7 (1) (2013) 317–326.

[37] P. Ramzi, F. Samadzadegan, P. Reinartz, Classification of hyperspectral data using an AdaBoostSVM technique applied on band clusters, IEEE Journal of Selected Topics in Applied Earth Observations and Remote Sensing 7 (6) (2013) 2066–2079.

[38] W. Li, S. Prasad, J.E. Fowler, Hyperspectral image classification using Gaussian mixture models and Markov random fields, IEEE Geoscience and Remote Sensing Letters 11 (1) (2013) 153–157.

[39] M. Khodadadzadeh, J. Li, A. Plaza, J. Bioucas-Dias, A subspace-based multinomial logistic regression for hyperspectral image classification, IEEE Geoscience and Remote Sensing Letters 11 (12) (2014) 2105–2109.

[40] W. Li, S. Prasad, J.E. Fowler, L.M. Bruce, Locality-preserving dimensionality reduction and classification for hyperspectral image analysis, IEEE Transactions on Geoscience and Remote Sensing 50 (4) (2011) 1185–1198.

[41] Y. Chen, Z. Lin, X. Zhao, G. Wang, Y. Gu, Deep learning-based classification of hyperspectral data, IEEE Journal of Selected Topics in Applied Earth Observations and Remote Sensing 7 (6) (2014) 2094–2107.

[42] Y. Liu, G. Cao, Q. Sun, M. Siegel, Hyperspectral classification via deep networks and superpixel segmentation, International Journal of Remote Sensing 36 (13) (2015) 3459–3482.

[43] W. Zhao, S. Du, Spectral–spatial feature extraction for hyperspectral image classification: A dimension reduction and deep learning approach, IEEE Transactions on Geoscience and Remote Sensing 54 (8) (2016) 4544–4554.

[44] M. Hall, E. Frank, G. Holmes, B. Pfahringer, P. Reutemann, I.H. Witten, The WEKA data mining software: an update, ACM SIGKDD Explorations Newsletter 11 (1) (2009) 10–18.

[45] N. Li, S. Takaki, Y. Tomiokay, H. Kitazawa, A multistage dataflow implementation of a deep convolutional neural network based on FPGA for high-speed object recognition, in: Proceedings of IEEE Southwest Symposium on Image Analysis and Interpretation, 2016, pp. 165–168.

[46] Z. Du, R. Fasthuber, T. Chen, P. Ienne, L. Li, T. Luo, X. Feng, Y. Chen, O. Temam, ShiDianNao: Shifting vision processing closer to the sensor, in: Proceedings of Annual International Symposium on Computer Architecture, 2015, pp. 92–104.

[47] P.-H. Pham, D. Jelaca, C. Farabet, B. Martini, Y. LeCun, E. Culurciello, NeuFlow: Dataflow vision processing system-on-a-chip, in: Proceedings of IEEE International Midwest Symposium on Circuits and Systems, 2012, pp. 1044–1047.

[48] L. Cavigelli, L. Benini, Origami: A 803 GOp/s/w convolutional network accelerator, IEEE Transactions on Circuits and Systems for Video Technology 27 (11) (2016) 2461–2475.

[49] R. Andri, L. Cavigelli, D. Rossi, L. Benini, YodaNN: An ultra-low power convolutional neural network accelerator based on binary weights, in: Proceedings of IEEE Computer Society Annual Symposium on Very Large Scale Integration, 2016, pp. 236–241.

CHAPTER 8

Hardware architecture optimization for object tracking

8.1 Background and challenges

This chapter is based on our related publication [1]. Object tracking is a very active field in computer vision. It is widely used in various applications, such as intelligent video monitoring, industrial automation, vehicle navigation, and robot control [2–4]. Many of those applications require real-time performance, which emerges as a challenge for edge computing or embedded platforms with limited computing and storage resources. Therefore it is urgent to customize a low-cost VLSI system for high-speed object tracking.

In recent years, many object tracking VLSI systems have been proposed [5–12]. However, most of them represent the object target only based on spatial textural features [5–9] and fail to make full use of the inherent motion information to ease the tracking procedure or improve the robustness against environmental variations. Some researchers have proposed an object tracking chip based on motion energy features [11] to boost tracking robustness. Extracting such motion features is computationally intensive via a stack of 3D spatiotemporal Gabor filters, requiring a huge amount of computing and memory resources, which are not plausible for edge or embedded applications. To realize flexible and robust tracking, some VLSI chips adopt hardware-algorithm codesign paradigm with an on-chip microprocessor unit (MPU) [5,11]. A significant part of the tracking workload is carried out by the MPU software in serial processing, causing performance bottleneck. To overcome this problem, some works massively employ parallel array coprocessors to improve processing speed to >1000 frame/s [9,10]. However, such fine-grained parallel processors consume a huge amount of computing resources and occupy high memory bandwidth. They do not fit low-cost edge computing or embedded systems.

In this chapter, we introduce a low-cost high-speed object tracking VLSI system with unified textural and dynamic compressive features to represent the target for robust tracking via fast elliptic template matching. Dynamic motion features are extracted via simple spatiotemporal filtering:

Deep Learning on Edge Computing Devices
https://doi.org/10.1016/B978-0-32-385783-3.00017-X
139

2D spatial DoG filtering followed by parameterized pixelwise temporal high-pass filtering, which is simple and configurable to adapt to different motion scenes. We evaluate the order of filters to optimize memory requirement, improve the VLSI system performance, and save hardware resources as much as possible.

- We use a memory-centric VLSI architecture with moderate memory consumption and only a few computational units, since computational units are much more expensive than memories for modern nanometer semiconductor technology.
- We introduce multiple-level pipelines and parallel processing circuits throughout feature extraction, target template matching, and template updating to improve system throughput.
- Careful designs and optimizations are carried out to further reduce the resource consumption of computational circuits.

8.2 Algorithm

8.2.1 Object tracking algorithm

Fig. 8.1 illustrates the proposed object tracking algorithm for high-speed low-cost VLSI implementation. Assume that the size and the position of the target in the first frame are known. For each new frame, a pixelwise temporal high-pass filter is applied to obtain the motion information [12],

$$\mathbf{H}[t] = c\mathbf{H}[t-1] + (1+c)(\mathbf{P}[t] - \mathbf{P}[t-1])/2, \qquad (8.1)$$

where $\mathbf{P}$ and $\mathbf{H}$ represent the input and high-pass filtered images, respectively, $0 < c < 1$ is the filter coefficient configurable for various motion scenes, and t denotes the discrete frame time. A spatial 2D Difference of Gaussian (DoG) filter is a precedent for suppressing high-frequency noises and the spatial DC component, which may interfere the motion features under a changing illumination.

Then we extract the textural and dynamic compressive features of samples (i.e., image regions with the same size of the target) from the original and filtered images, respectively. Each compressive feature component is the difference of the pixel intensity summations across a pair of rectangular patches within the sample region. The offset and scale of each patch are randomly selected before tracking and kept unchanged throughout. The same set of these patch parameters applies to all samples. Our unified compressive feature vector is the concatenation of the textural and dynamic

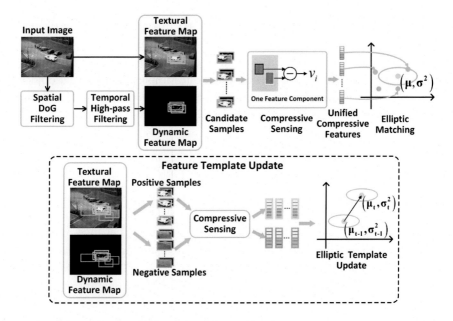

Figure 8.1 Our proposed object tracking algorithm flow.

compressive features. The features can be quickly calculated via integral image [13]. The integral image $\mathbf{IP}(x, y)$ of the image $\mathbf{P}(x, y)$ is defined and computed via an iteration as

$$\mathbf{IP}(x, y) = \sum_{b=0}^{y} \sum_{a=0}^{x} \mathbf{P}(a, b) \tag{8.2}$$
$$= \mathbf{IP}(x, y - 1) + \mathbf{IP}(x - 1, y) - \mathbf{IP}(x - 1, y - 1) + \mathbf{P}(x, y),$$

where $\mathbf{IP} = 0$ if $x < 0$ or $y < 0$. Thus one feature component v from two patches $(x_l^{(g)}, x_r^{(g)}, y_u^{(d)}, y_d^{(g)})$ $(g = 1, 2$, the subscripts l/r and u/d denote the leftmost/rightmost column and the uppermost/downmost row of the patch, respectively) on the image $\mathbf{P}(x, y)$ can be simply obtained by merely eight add/sub operations:

$$v = \sum_{b=y_u^{(1)}}^{y_d^{(1)}} \sum_{a=x_l^{(1)}}^{x_r^{(1)}} \mathbf{P}(x, y) - \sum_{b=y_u^{(2)}}^{y_d^{(2)}} \sum_{a=x_l^{(2)}}^{x_r^{(2)}} \mathbf{P}(x, y) \tag{8.3}$$
$$= (\mathbf{IP}(x_r^{(1)}, y_d^{1}) - \mathbf{IP}(x_l^{(1)} - 1, y_d^{(1)}) - \mathbf{IP}(x_r^{(1)}, y_u^{(1)} - 1)$$
$$+ \mathbf{IP}(x_l^{(1)} - 1, y_u^{(1)} - 1)) + (-\mathbf{IP}(x_r^{(2)}, y_d^{2}) + \mathbf{IP}(x_l^{(2)} - 1, y_d^{(2)})$$
$$+ \mathbf{IP}(x_r^{(2)}, y_u^{(2)} - 1) - \mathbf{IP}(x_l^{(2)} - 1, y_u^{(2)} - 1)).$$

To predict the target position in the current frame, we compute the unified compressive features of the samples surrounding the target position of the previous frame and employ an elliptic feature template matching procedure. The matching degree between one sample and the target object is measured as the ratio of the elliptic distances between the sample and the positive/negative templates (to be explained soon) as

$$S = \frac{\sum_{m=1}^{M}(v_m - \mu_m^p)^2/(\sigma_m^p)^2}{\sum_{m=1}^{M}(v_m - \mu_m^n)^2/(\sigma_m^n)^2}, \tag{8.4}$$

where M is the unified feature vector dimension, v_m is the mth component of the sample feature vector, (μ_m, σ_m) is the mth component of the template, and the superscript p/n denotes the positive/negative template. The low computational overhead of the elliptic matching is essential to ensuring real-time low-cost hardware implementation. The combination of both object and background contexts improves tracking stability and accuracy.

To update the templates online, we draw positive samples uniformly centered at a circle of radius R1 near current target position and negative samples (backgrounds) uniformly centered in a ring area of inner radius R2 and outer radius R3 that are sufficiently far away from the target position. The number of both positive and negative samples is set to $K = 2^5 = 32$, allowing us to replace expensive hardware dividers by much simpler right-shifters. The positive/negative templates follow the same update strategy by using extracted unified compressive features from respective positive/negative samples as

$$\mu_m[t] = \gamma\mu_m[t-1] + \frac{1-\gamma}{K}\sum_{k=1}^{K}v_m[k][t], \tag{8.5}$$

$$\sigma_m^2[t] = \frac{\gamma}{K}\sum_{k=1}^{K}\left(v_m[k][t-1] - \mu_m[t]\right)^2 + \frac{1-\gamma}{K}\sum_{k=1}^{K}\left(v_m[k][t] - \mu_m[t]\right)^2,$$

where k is the sample index, and $0 < \gamma < 1$ is the updating rate.

8.2.2 Memory optimization for spatiotemporal filtering

To extract the unified compressive features, we can naturally arrange the spatiotemporal filtering order as mentioned above: spatial 2-D DoG filtering, temporal high-pass filtering and image integration (D–H–I Sequence).

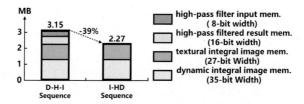

Figure 8.2 Comparison of estimated memory costs for two filtering sequences.

Thus two memory blocks are required to buffer the original image and the temporal high-pass filtered image (i.e., the **P** and **H** images in Eq. (8.1)) for subsequent usage and other two banks for textural and dynamic integral images. The DoG filter does not require an image buffer in a pixel stream processing architecture, as will be illustrated in Section 8.3. Indeed, a large amount of memory requirements can be optimized out if we carefully arrange the filtering sequence by fully leveraging the linearity of all the filters involved. In light of this, we have finally found the optimal I–HD sequence: computing the integral image of the input and then performing the temporal high-pass filtering with the spatial DoG filter embedded in it as

$$\mathbf{IH}[t] = c\mathbf{IH}[t-1] + (1+c)\,\text{DoG}((\mathbf{IP}[t] - \mathbf{IP}[t-1])/2), \qquad (8.6)$$

where **IP** denotes the integral of the original input image (i.e., the textural integral image), and **IH** is the dynamic integral image. This way, **IP** can be reused for both textural and dynamic feature extractions, and we only need two memory banks to buffer the **IP** and **IH** images. We have estimated the memory consumption on the two filtering sequences for typical $640 \times 480 \times 8$-bit images in Fig. 8.2. The I–HD sequence saves $\sim$39% memory resources.

8.3 Hardware implementation and optimization

8.3.1 VLSI architecture

Fig. 8.3 shows the proposed object tracking VLSI system architecture. The feature extracting block includes an image integrator and a configurable spatiotemporal filter, which is a pixelwise temporal high-pass filter tightly embedding a spatial DoG filter. The feature matching block consists of a matching engine and an updating engine for the feature templates. These computational blocks are optimized and minimized to build a

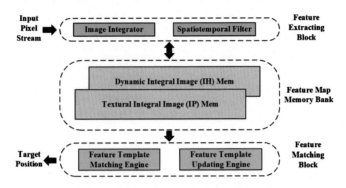

Figure 8.3 The proposed object tracking VLSI architecture.

low-cost memory-centric architecture, as memory cells are much cheaper than computing resources in modern nanometer semiconductor technology. Multiple-level pipelines and parallel processing circuits are adopted to improve the system throughput with such minimized computing resources.

8.3.2 Block circuit design

To reduce system cost while realizing fine-grained pipelines with parallel circuits to boost processing speed, we carefully design and optimize the computational block circuits. Fig. 8.4 shows the circuit details of the feature extracting block, which is based on a pixel stream processing structure to minimize computational units, at a matched rate of real-time image sensors [12].

Fig. 8.4(a) is the input image integrator. A row buffer is used to cache one row of the latest obtained pixels of current integral image for iterative usage. A 4-input adder calculates the integral image following Eq. (8.2). It can produce one IP pixel per clock cycle.

Fig. 8.4(b) shows the circuit of the pixelwise temporal high-pass filter embedding the spatial DoG filter, which computes Eq. (8.6). The filter coefficient c is unsigned 8-bit and can be configured to flexibly adjust the pass band to adapt to various motion scenarios. The filter receives the unsigned 32-bit pixel stream of the textural integral image (**IP**) from the image integrator, generates a signed 40-bit (including 8-bit fractional) pixel stream of the dynamic integral image (**IH**), and updates the **IP** and **IH** memories along the streams. It uses a 10-stage (one clock cycle per stage) pixel-level pipeline to realize the pixel stream processing and match the high throughput of the image integrator.

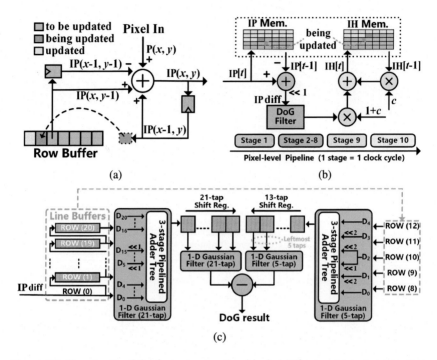

Figure 8.4 The circuits of the feature extracting block. (a) The input image integrator. (b) The pixelwise spatiotemporal filter. (c) Further expansion of the spatial 2-D DoG filter circuit embedded inside the spatiotemporal filter.

The 7-stage pipelined DoG filter circuit is further expanded in Fig. 8.4(c). It computes the difference between the results of two spatial 2-D Gaussian filters with different cut-off frequencies and kernel sizes. The line buffers cache the latest rows of the $(\mathbf{IP}[t] - \mathbf{IP}[t-1])/2$ pixel stream and are shared among the two parallel Gaussian filters. Moreover, each 2-D Gaussian filter core is decomposed into horizontal and vertical 1-D Gaussian filters to save computing resources [12]. The 1-D Gaussian weights are optimized and restricted to be among the set of 1, 2, 4, 6. So, convolving the input image with such filter weights can be easily accomplished via simple bit-shifters and adders, instead of expensive multipliers.

A 3-stage pipelined adder tree is used in each 1-D Gaussian filter. Note that the feature extracting block is only responsible for producing and caching the **IP** and **IH** integral image maps, as the compressive features can be obtained via a few simple operations on the integral images by the feature matching block on-the-fly when it accesses these memories during feature matching and template updating. This computing-upon-request

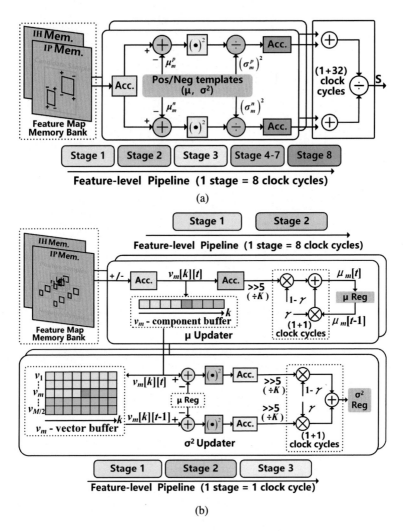

Figure 8.5 The circuits of the feature matching block. (a) The feature template matching engine. (b) The feature template updating engine.

paradigm eliminates the memory and time overheads for a large group of compressive feature vectors of the candidate samples and the positive/negative samples.

Fig. 8.5(a) is the circuit of the feature template matching engine computing Eq. (8.4). A region of 20×20 pixels centered at the tracked target in the previous frame is used to search for the target in current frame. Each pixel location in this region is treated as the center of a candidate sample for the target. The matching engine has an 8-stage feature-level pipeline to accelerate the computations for the summation terms in the dividend and the divisor of Eq. (8.4). One pipeline stage contains eight clock cycles. As described above, the compressive features are serially computed on demand from the integral images, which is done in eight clock cycles by the accumulator in the first pipeline stage. The dividers occupy four stages and are always busy when the pipeline works. The other components occupy one stage each, but are only busy for one clock cycle in their respective stage. After the pipeline, 33 extra clock cycles are needed for computing the final result of Eq. (8.4). The operations along textural and dynamic feature dimensions and along positive and negative templates are parallelized to further improve processing speed.

Fig. 8.5(b) shows the circuit of the feature template updating engine computing Eq. (8.5), with a similar pipeline and parallel structure. In our design, R1, R2, and R3 are set to 4, 15, and 25, respectively, and $0 < \gamma < 1$ is coded as an unsigned 8-bit fractional. This engine updates template parameters μ_m and σ_m^2 in a dimensionwise way on extracted features across all positive and negative samples. It has a two-stage (8 clock cycles per stage) feature-level pipeline for μ_m and a three-stage (1 clock cycle per stage) feature-level pipeline for σ_m^2. Updates are carried out in parallel between textural and dynamic dimensions and between μ_m and σ_m^2 though a small lag exists there as renewing σ_m^2 requires updated μ_m.

8.4 Application experiments

In this section, we conducted an experiment in software simulation to demonstrate the efficacy of our proposed unified compressive features for robust tracking: using sole textural compressive features, using sole dynamic compressive features, and using the proposed unified textural and dynamic compressive features.

Fig. 8.6(a) shows a dynamic compressive feature map (i.e., the **IH** integral image) with the spatiotemporal filter coefficient set to $c = 187 \times 2^{-8}$. There is a car moving from right to left in Fig. 8.6(a), and it was well captured by the dynamic feature map. Figs. 8.6(b) and (c) use videos with no and remarkable ambient illumination changes, respectively. The tracking results in Fig. 8.6(b) using the three feature representations are close to each other. However, in Fig. 8.6(c) the tracking results with sole textural or dynamic compressive features exhibit large deviations, whereas the unified

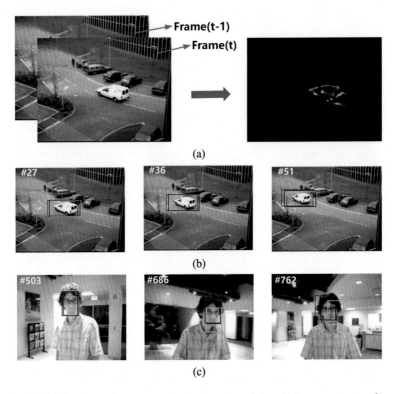

Figure 8.6 (a) the dynamic compressive feature map. (b) and (c) comparisons of tracking results under three feature representations: Sole Textural Compressive Features (STCF-red), Sole Dynamic Compressive Features (SDCF-green), and our Unified Textural and Dynamic Compressive Features (UTDCF-blue).

compressive features still work properly. This demonstrates the robustness of unified compressive features against illumination changes.

An FPGA prototype of the proposed object tracking VLSI system was implemented on the ZC706 platform. For a typical input image resolution of 320 × 240, the FPGA resource consumption is listed in Table 8.1. The logic resource consumption is very small, and memory consumption is moderate. The memory usages increase with the image resolution, because textural and dynamic integration images need to be stored. However, the manufacturing cost for semiconductor memories under modern nanotechnology is much less than that of logic resources. The more memory consumption due to higher image resolution does not increase the overall system cost drastically. The prototype runs at a 100-MHz clock frequency,

Table 8.1 FPGA resource utilization for 320 × 240 resolution.

Device	Slice Reg	Slice LUTs	DSPs	Block RAM
Zynq-7045	16947 (3.9%)	20873 (9.5%)	48 (5.3%)	161 (29.5%)

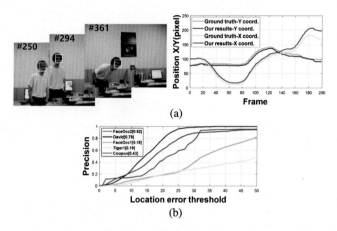

(a)

(b)

Figure 8.7 Experimental results on our FPGA prototype of the tracking VLSI system. (a) A sample video result. (b) The tracking precisions on five OTB videos. The particular precision metrics under the commonly used threshold of 20 pixels are stated in the legend.

which is equivalent to 600 frames/s for 320 × 240 images. Its peak power consumption is 768 mW (estimated by the Xilinx Vivado tool).

Fig. 8.7(a) gives a qualitative tracking result of the prototype on a sample video from the OTB dataset. The tracked object positions basically keep up with the ground truth. Fig. 8.7(b) demonstrates quantitative results on five more OTB videos. The precision means the percentage of correctly tracked frames in the whole video. If the distance (in terms of pixels) between the object position predicted by our prototype and the ground truth is above a certain threshold in one frame, then this frame is regarded as incorrectly tracked [8]. Table 8.2 further compares the tracking precisions of our system and those of the hardware implementation in [8] on the five videos. These results indicate that our system performs poorly on the Tiger1 and David videos. The two videos undergo fast scale changes or large occlusions, respectively, but our simple unified compressive features are not scale-invariant or scale-adaptive, and our fast template updating scheme cannot distinguish occlusions and freeze the target template before occlusion. Fig. 8.8 visualizes more tracking results comparing our system and state-of-the-art algorithms [14] on more OTB video clips. Although

Table 8.2 Precision comparison of hardware implementations (threshold = 20).

Video	David	FaceOcc1	FaceOcc2	Tiger1	Coupon
Ref. [8]	0.88	0.12	0.44	0.37	0.40
Ours	0.79	0.18	0.62	0.19	0.43

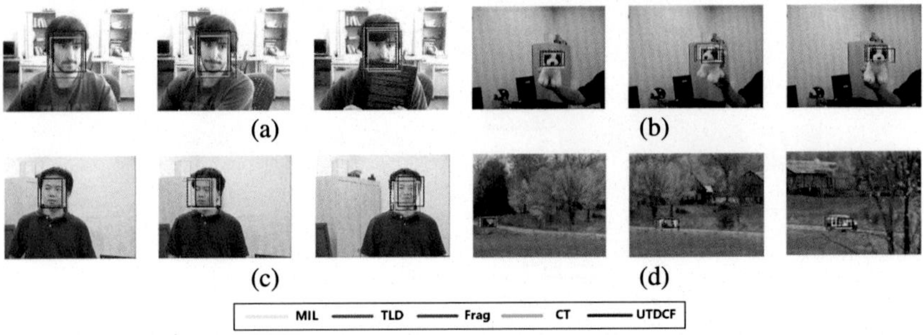

(a)   (b)

(c)   (d)

MIL ——— TLD ——— Frag ——— CT ——— UTDCF

Figure 8.8 Tracking result comparison between the proposed method and popular algorithms.

Fig. 8.8(a) sees a partial occlusion and Fig. 8.8(d) has small scale changes, the proposed method achieves good tracking performance in most frames.

Table 8.3 compares the proposed VLSI system to prior hardware designs [7–9,11,15]. The hardware system in [11] adopts hardware–software codesign, thereby suffering low frame rate. Using massively parallel array coprocessors in [9] achieves a very high frame rate of 1000 frames/s, but this leads to a huge consumption of computing resources and occupies high memory bandwidth, which is not suitable for embedded applications. In [15], complicated features are extracted to achieve robust tracking. It relies on expensive advanced ASIC technology to maintain real-time performance. The works [7–9,15] only employ spatial textural features to represent the target, without exploring the motion information of the target. Our VLSI system uses robust and computationally simple unified textural and dynamic compressive features to represent the target and achieves robust tracking at a relatively high frame rate of 600 frames/s while only consuming a few logic resources and a moderate amount of memory resources. Compared to complicated tracking methods [15,16], our simple tracking algorithm facilitates high-speed and low-cost hardware implementations desired by edge-computing devices and embedded systems, but at the cost of sacrificing adaptation to fast scale changes or large occlusions during tracking, as illustrated by Fig. 8.7(b) and Table 8.2. This is the primary application limitation of our hardware system.

Table 8.3 Comparisons of object tracking hardware implementations.

	Feature	Frame rate (frames/s)	Image reso.	Clock Freq. (MHz)	Power effi. (nJ/pixel)
Stratix-III [8]	Directional Edge	150	640 × 480	60	N/A
Arria-V[9]	Gray-Level LBP	2800	128 × 128	100	N/A
28nm ASIC [15]	Opticalflow+Depth	30	1920 × 1080	180	12.22
Virtex-4 [7]	LBP+HOG	60	640 × 480	25	N/A
Virtex-5 [11]	Oriented energy	30	640 × 480	24	N/A
Zynq-7045 (ours)	UTDCF	630 / 253	320 × 240 / 640 × 480	100	15.87

This chapter presents a low-cost high-speed object VLSI system based on simple and robust unified textural and dynamic compressive features and elliptic matching. The system architecture uses a memory-centric paradigm, multiple-level pipelines, and parallel processing circuits to improve tracking speed while reducing hardware costs as much as possible. An FPGA prototype of the proposed VLSI system was implemented with a few computational resources and a moderate memory consumption. It can process 320×240 resolution images at 600 frames/s under a 100-MHz clock frequency. Tracking results by the proposed prototype and comparisons to prior works demonstrate that our tracking system is suitable for high-speed low-cost embedded visual tracking applications.

References

[1] W. He, J. Zhang, Y. Lin, X. Zhou, P. Li, L. Liu, N. Wu, C. Shi, A low-cost high-speed object tracking VLSI system based on unified textural and dynamic compressive features, IEEE Transactions on Circuits and Systems. II, Express Briefs 68 (3) (2020) 1013–1017.

[2] A. Yilmaz, O. Javed, M. Shah, Object tracking: A survey, ACM Computing Surveys 38 (4) (2006).

[3] H. Yang, L. Shao, F. Zheng, L. Wang, Z. Song, Recent advances and trends in visual tracking: A review, Neurocomputing 74 (18) (2011) 3823–3831.

[4] J.K. Sunkara, M. Santhosh, S.B. Cherukuri, L.G. Krishna, Object tracking techniques and performance measures − a conceptual survey, in: Proceedings of International Conference on Power, Control, Signals and Instrumentation Engineering, 2017, pp. 2297–2305.

[5] S.-A. Li, C.-C. Hsu, W.-L. Lin, J.-P. Wang, Hardware/software co-design of particle filter and its application in object tracking, in: Proceedings of International Conference on System Science and Engineering, 2011, pp. 87–91.

[6] J.U. Cho, S.H. Jin, X. Dai Pham, J.W. Jeon, J.E. Byun, H. Kang, A real-time object tracking system using a particle filter, in: Proceedings of IEEE International Conference on Intelligent Robots and Systems, 2006, pp. 2822–2827.

[7] T. Sledeviè, A. Serackis, D. Plonis, FPGA-based selected object tracking using LBP, HOG and motion detection, in: Proceedings of IEEE Workshop on Advances in Information, Electronic and Electrical Engineering, 2018, pp. 1–5.

[8] P. Zhao, H. Zhu, H. Li, T. Shibata, A directional-edge-based real-time object tracking system employing multiple candidate-location generation, IEEE Transactions on Circuits and Systems for Video Technology 23 (3) (2012) 503–517.

[9] Y. Yang, J. Yang, L. Liu, N. Wu, High-speed target tracking system based on a hierarchical parallel vision processor and gray-level LBP algorithm, IEEE Transactions on Systems, Man, and Cybernetics: Systems 47 (6) (2016) 950–964.

[10] J. Yang, C. Shi, L. Liu, N. Wu, Heterogeneous vision chip and LBP-based algorithm for high-speed tracking, Electronics Letters 50 (6) (2014) 438–439.

[11] E. Norouznezhad, A. Bigdeli, A. Postula, B.C. Lovell, Robust object tracking using local oriented energy features and its hardware/software implementation, in: Proceedings of International Conference on Control, Automation, Robotics and Vision, 2010, pp. 2060–2066.

[12] C. Shi, G. Luo, A streaming motion magnification core for smart image sensors, IEEE Transactions on Circuits and Systems. II, Express Briefs 65 (9) (2017) 1229–1233.

[13] K. Zhang, L. Zhang, M.-H. Yang, Fast compressive tracking, IEEE Transactions on Pattern Analysis and Machine Intelligence 36 (10) (2014) 2002–2015.

[14] Visual tracker benchmark, URL http://www.visual-tracking.net.

[15] Z. Li, J. Wang, D. Sylvester, D. Blaauw, H.S. Kim, A 1920 × 1080 25-frames/s 2.4-tops/w low-power 6-d vision processor for unified optical flow and stereo depth with semi-global matching, IEEE Journal of Solid-State Circuits 54 (4) (2019) 1048–1058.

[16] B. Chen, D. Wang, P. Li, S. Wang, H. Lu, Real-time 'actor-critic' tracking, in: Proceedings of European Conference on Computer Vision, 2018, pp. 318–334.

CHAPTER 9

SensCamera: A learning-based smart camera prototype

9.1 Challenges beyond pattern recognition

With the advances in the technology of integrated circuits and embedded computing, wireless smart cameras with powerful object detection function have been widely employed for different applications [1,2]. As one of the state-of-the-art methods, the convolutional neural network (CNN) has been proven to be a great success for object detection, arousing a growth of interest to implement the convolutional neural network-based smart cameras for different applications such as intrusion detection [3–5].

Early object detection approaches based on the convolutional neural network consist of a region extraction stage to select thousands of regions from the target image for object detection, which would lead to high computational overhead, such as the famous Regional CNN (R-CNN) [6]. Recently, a set of efficient object detection convolutional neural network architectures were proposed, including the Fast R-CNN [7], the Faster R-CNN [8], the Single Shot Detection (SSD) [9], and the YOLO models [10]. Inspired by these works, the computational complexity of the CNN-based object detection has been greatly reduced, which makes it feasible to implement CNN-based computer vision applications using wireless embedded devices.

Research [11] pioneered the use of convolution operations for compressive sensing, but it still used random sensing matrices to ensure the incoherence condition. Recently, a set of learning-based methods used a group of training samples to estimate the deterministic sensing matrices. As an early attempt, the NuMax method can estimate the linear near-isometric sensing matrix by solving the semidefinite program (SDP) problem [12]. Baldassarre et al. [13] proposed a learning-based subsampling method that can estimate the sensing matrix by solving combinatorial optimization problems. Blasiok et al. [14] relaxed the NuMax SDP problem as an eigenvalue problem and proposed ADAGIO method for a larger data set containing thousands of samples.

Recently, some researchers attempted to use convolutional neural networks to solve different problems of compressive sensing. Mousavi et

Deep Learning on Edge Computing Devices
https://doi.org/10.1016/B978-0-32-385783-3.00018-1

al. [15] proposed to use a convolutional neural network to recover the original signal from random under-sampled measurements. Later, Mousavi et al. [16] improved their method by using a convolutional neural network to compress and recover the signal. Lu et al. [17] proposed a similar idea for image compression. Iliadis et al. [18] proposed to use a deep fully connected network for video image recovery. Ren et al. [19] proposed a progressive reconstruction method following the concept of the Laplacian pyramid. Wu et al. [20] improved the performance and speed of reconstruction via metalearning. Chen et al. [21] adopted multilayer residual coding scheme to improve rate-distortion performance of compressive sensing-based image coding. Zhou et al. [22] developed a multichannel deep network for block-based image compressive sensing by exploiting interblock correlation. The main difference between our proposed method and these researches is that the Compressive Convolutional Network (CCN) is not a network built for image compression or recovery, but a network enhancement method that enables the object detection network to gain the capability of image compression without degrading performance.

Object detection-based smart cameras have been applied to many internet of things (IoT) scenarios, such as home [23], traffic [24], factories [25], and parking lots [4,26], where big data are commonly encountered. Therefore only those interesting frames should be transmitted. In this case, detection is needed to find those interesting frames, whereas image compression is needed for data transmission. For example, in the home monitoring, most of the time the camera should not transmit the normal images to houseowner unless certain events are detected, such as an intrusion, people falling, etc. Moreover, in the factory quality inspection line, the cameras are deployed for quality inspection. They also only transmit the image information when the unqualified products are detected.

From a system point of view, the wireless smart camera is usually implemented using reconfigurable Field Programmable Gate Arrays (FPGAs) and System on Chips (SoCs). Several hardware-accelerated embedded systems have been introduced for CNN-based image classification applications during the last few years [27–31]. However, unlike the image classification task, object detection is much more computation-intensive and energy-consuming since a large number of possible object proposals need to be evaluated. Only until very recently could researchers manage to implement light-weight CNN-based object detection algorithms using embedded systems [32,33].

A traditional approach to achieve image compression is using additional logic devices, like image/video coding approaches [34–37], which potentially increase the cost and computation complexity at the system level. To address the challenge, in this paper, we propose an efficient method for unified object detection and image compression. The basic idea is optimizing and reusing the convolution operation of the convolutional neural network to perform feature extraction and image compression simultaneously; therefore there is no requirement for extra computational overhead, saving the cost and computation occupation of wireless computer vision applications.

The proposed approach is based on the modern compressive sensing technique. By solving undetermined linear systems it has been proved that the sparsity of the image signal makes it possible to be recovered from fewer samples [38]. To recover a compressed image, the theory of compressive sensing requires a sufficient incoherence condition, which is applied through the *isometric property* [39,40]. At the front end, traditional compressive sensing methods use random matrices for data embedding, which can meet incoherence conditions with high probability [41–44].

It is not trivial to incorporate the compressive sensing in the deep learning framework. The proposed incoherent convolution operation is deterministic and can be learned from samples, which is different from the work of random convolution operation [11]. To accurately recover the image, the incoherent condition must be satisfied, so the proposed method defines a relaxed measurement of the mutual coherence between the sensing and basis matrices. By minimizing the coherence measurement in the regularized training process the original image can be compressed with higher quality. Compared to our conference version [45], this paper is much more comprehensive, which features the hardware and system-level innovation, and covers the design work of the wireless smart camera prototype for video surveillance application. Fig. 9.1 illustrates the typical object detection application implemented using the prototyping wireless smart camera we built. The prototype is named as SensCamera.

From an algorithmic point of view, there are several *advantages* for adopting the incoherent convolution approach. First, through learning near-isometric sensing matrix from a large-scale training set, the reconstructed peak signal-to-noise ratio (PSNR) of the compressed images is 2.7–5.2 dB higher than that of the standard JPEG and traditional compressive sensing methods [14,46]. Secondly, since the neural network inference stage has no computational overhead and no additional latency, the proposed method

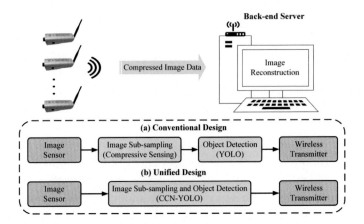

Figure 9.1 Typical scenario of applying wireless smart cameras for surveillance purpose. One or multiple camera systems can be deployed at the front end to perform image acquisition, compression, and object detection. The compressed sequential images are transmitted through WIFI to the back-end server, where images are decompressed for visualization and further analysis.

has an efficiency improvement of more than $3\times$ compared with traditional methods [13]. Thirdly, it is based on backpropagation used to train deep neural networks, so it is significantly more efficient than the NuMax [12] and ADAGIO [14] algorithms to estimate near–isometric sensing matrix. The proposed method extends the data–driven compressive sensing method to large–scale data sets.

From a system point of view, there are two main advantages for applying the SensCamera. First, by supporting object detection at the front end the smart camera only has to activate wireless image transmission when a certain event was detected. For the example of typical face detection applications, the SensCamera prototype only starts to transmit image frames when human faces are detected, which can dramatically save communication traffic and data storage requirement. Secondly, the SensCamera can compress the detected video images without computational overhead, which further improves computation efficiency. The whole system consists of one or multiple wireless cameras and a postprocessing computer, which receives the compressed images from the cameras through the WIFI transmitter.

The main contributions are as follows.

- A novel hardware-friendly compressive convolution network (CCN) is proposed, which can simultaneously achieve object detection and image compression in one network.

- A novel incoherent convolution regularization is presented for learning the sensing matrix to achieve the near-isometric property of compressive sensing.
- An efficient prototyping wireless smart camera (SensCamera) is designed, which can compress video images and reduce transmission consumption without introducing additional computational overhead.

9.2 Compressive convolutional network model

The SensCamera is designed to perform object detection and image compression via a pretrained convolutional neural network, which is implemented and accelerated by one dedicated FPGA device. To reduce computational overhead, power consumption and communication bandwidth, we invent a compressive-sensing-enabled convolutional neural network, which can reuse the convolution operation for image compression and feature extraction. At the beginning, we briefly introduce the standard compressive sensing approach.

9.2.1 Standard compressive sensing

Compressive sensing is a low-rate sampling approach for the signals that are known to be sparse. Suppose the signal $\mathbf{x}$ is an N-dimensional vector, which can be sampled using a *sensing matrix* $\Phi \in \mathbb{R}^{M \times N}$ as

$$\mathbf{y} = \Phi \mathbf{x}. \tag{9.1}$$

The constant M determines the sampling rate. Because M is smaller than N in compressive sensing, Eq. (9.1) is underdetermined, and the signal $\mathbf{x}$ cannot be uniquely recovered from Φ and $\mathbf{y}$. However, the assumption of sparsity allows the signal $\mathbf{x}$ to be represented using a set of sparse coefficient $\mathbf{s} \in \mathbb{R}^N$ and a matrix of basis $\Psi \in \mathbb{R}^{N \times N}$ as $\mathbf{x} = \Psi \mathbf{s}$. Then we have $\mathbf{y} = \Phi \Psi \mathbf{s} = \Theta \mathbf{s}$, where $\Theta = \Phi \Psi$ is an $M \times N$ measurement matrix. Since $\mathbf{s}$ is sparse, it is possible to retrieve the value of $\mathbf{s}$ by solving the L1 norm minimization problem as

$$\mathbf{s} = \min_{\mathbf{s}} \|\mathbf{s}\|_1, \quad \text{s.t.} \ \|\mathbf{y} - \Theta \mathbf{s}\|_2 < \xi. \tag{9.2}$$

After solving Eq. (9.2), we can approximate the original signal $\mathbf{x}$ by $\hat{\mathbf{x}} = \Psi \mathbf{s}$.

Generally, based on Eqs. (9.1) and (9.2), one of the main goals of compressive sensing is to learn the *sensing matrix* Φ. Researches mainly focus on two points.

1. **The incoherence condition.** To find the unique sparest solution of Eq. (9.2), Φ should be built to satisfy the incoherence condition, i.e., the matrices Φ and Ψ should be incoherent [47].
2. **The deterministic sensing matrix.** In practice, we can use either random or deterministic sensing matrix Φ. For the random approach, it is proven that the matrix with Gaussian entries satisfies the incoherence condition. However, recent researches showed that by learning deterministic sensing matrix from data the compressed images can be reconstructed with higher quality [13].

Our proposed method attempts to find the optimal sensing matrix Φ to satisfy the incoherent condition with given basis matrix Ψ, e.g., a discrete wavelet transform (DWT) matrix. We calculate the near-isometric sensing matrix by data-driven deep learning approach.

9.2.2 The framework of compressive convolutional network

The goal of object detection is recognizing multiple objects in a single image. The class confidence and the bounding box for each object are returned. So far, many convolutional neural network-based frameworks have been proposed for object detection [8–10]. Different frameworks usually have different types of layers and different parameters, yet a typical convolutional neural network framework uses a pipeline of modules for image classification and object detection.

Fig. 9.2 shows the framework of our proposed CCN model mainly including two branches, image compression and object detection. The object detection branch is with the standard convolutional neural network, such as YOLOv2 [10], including twenty-three conventional convolutional layers, one reorganizing layer, five max-pooling layers, and one soft-max layer. The image compression branch includes one *compressive convolutional* layer and one uniform pooling layer with quantization operation. Based on the object detection results, the compressed image data, along with the class confidence and bounding box of each object, can be transmitted to the back-end server for the subsequent tasks.

We innovatively reuse *the first layer* of the object detection convolutional neural network model as the *compressive convolutional* layer to perform image compression. Note that our proposed image compression branch can be incorporated into any convolution neural networks designed for all kinds of applications, e.g., detection, classification, segmentation, etc.

From a functional point of view, the proposed CCN performs image compression and object detection simultaneously at the inference stage.

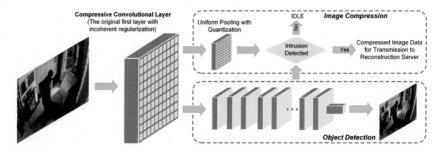

Figure 9.2 The prototyping Compressive Convolutional Network built for unified object detection and image compression. Compared to the standard convolutional neural network-based object detection models, the first convolutional layer is modified and optimized for recoverable data embedding and image compression. The output of the Compressive Convolutional Layer associated with the optimal kernel was subsampled and quantized, which is used as the compressed image data, and transmitted to backend server for image reconstruction when certain event such as an intrusion is detected.

Specifically, given a test image, the uniform pooling layer, built after the compressive convolutional layer, subsamples the image features. Then we adopt the DSQ quantization method to transform the subsampled features into fixed-point representation [48]. The compressed features can be used both for object detection and image recovery.

The main difference between the proposed method and other CNN-based frameworks is in the compressive convolutional layer, which is the first layer of the original framework. Our proposed compressive convolutional layer (CCL) is basically a 3×3 convolutional layer, which is optimized for compressive sensing. As a data-driven approach, the CCL uses the deterministic convolution operation for recoverable data embedding. The convolution operation is optimized to fulfill the incoherence condition so that the sampled feature maps can be used to reconstruct the original image by reconstruction algorithms like the orthogonal matching pursuit [49].

9.2.3 Data embedding via convolution operation

In this subsection, we focus on estimating the deterministic sensing matrix. As shown in [11], the convolution operation can be seen as a linear embedding operation. Let $\mathbf{W} \in \mathbb{R}^{3 \times 3}$ be a kernel matrix of the compressive convolutional layer, and let $\mathbf{X} \in \mathbb{R}^{P \times Q}$ be any channel of the input image data. Given $N = P \times Q$, $\mathbf{X}$ can be vectorized and represented as $\mathbf{x} \in \mathbb{R}^N$. Since the convolution operation $\otimes$ in the convolutional neural network only consists of first-order multiplications, it can be reformulated as a linear embedding operation as

$$\text{vec}(\mathbf{W} * \mathbf{X}) \doteq \Phi \mathbf{x} = \mathbf{y}, \qquad (9.3)$$

where $*$ is the convolution operation, $\text{vec}(\cdot)$ is the vectorization operation, $\Phi \in \mathbb{R}^{N \times N}$ is the associated square embedding matrix determined by
the kernel matrix $\mathbf{W}$, and $\mathbf{y}$ is the vectorized output of the convolution
operation.

Since the kernel matrices in the convolutional neural network model
are learned from training samples, the sensing matrix Φ is determined by
iterative training. Define the column vector $\mathbf{w} \in \mathbb{R}^{2Q+3}$ based on the kernel
matrix $\mathbf{W}$ as $\mathbf{w}^{\mathrm{T}} = [w_1, w_2, w_3, \mathbf{0}, w_4, w_5, w_6, \mathbf{0}, w_7, w_8, w_9]$, where $w_1, \dots, w_9$
are the nine elements of the kernel matrix $\mathbf{W}$. The embedding matrix
associated with the kernel can be written as

$$\Phi = \begin{pmatrix} \mathbf{w}^{\mathrm{T}} & \mathbf{0} & \dots & \mathbf{0} & \mathbf{0} \\ \mathbf{0} & \mathbf{w}^{\mathrm{T}} & \dots & \mathbf{0} & \mathbf{0} \\ \vdots & & \dots & & \vdots \\ \mathbf{0} & \mathbf{0} & \dots & \mathbf{w}^{\mathrm{T}} & \mathbf{0} \\ \mathbf{0} & \mathbf{0} & \dots & \mathbf{0} & \mathbf{w}^{\mathrm{T}} \end{pmatrix}_{N \times N}, \qquad (9.4)$$

where $\mathbf{0}$ and 0 are the *row* vector of zeros and the scalar zero. The embedding matrix Φ is a sparse matrix with 3×3 nonzero elements in each
row.

It is worth noting that Eqs. (9.3) and (9.1) have the same linear form, but
different from the standard compressive sensing, the convolution operation
of the convolutional neural network does not reduce the dimension of the
data. To compress the image to dimension M ($M \ll N$), a *uniform-pooling
layer* is inserted after the compressive convolutional layer for dimension
reduction. In practice, a single feature map is selected for subsampling, and
$M \times N$ elements are uniformly extracted in a row-by-row fashion with
equal probability.

9.2.4 Coherence regularization

In this subsection, we focus on addressing the incoherence condition. As a
data–driven approach, Eq. (9.3) uses deterministic sensing matrix Φ learned
from samples. According to the theorem of compressive sensing, Φ should
satisfy the incoherence condition that the sensing matrix Φ and the basis
matrix Ψ are incoherent. Let $\boldsymbol{\varphi}_i^{\mathrm{T}}$ be the ith row of Φ, and let $\boldsymbol{\psi}_j$ be the jth

column of Ψ. The mutual coherence between Φ and Ψ is defined as

$$\mu(\Phi, \Psi) = \max | < \boldsymbol{\varphi}_i, \boldsymbol{\psi}_j > | = \max |\boldsymbol{\varphi}_i^T \boldsymbol{\psi}_j|. \tag{9.5}$$

Within the compressive sensing framework, low coherence between Φ and Ψ translates to fewer samples required for recovering the signal. For data-driven approaches, it is intuitive to minimize the mutual coherence during the training process. However, since the mutual coherence in Eq. (9.5) is not differentiable, we relax it as the following form:

$$\mathcal{R}_{\mathbf{W}}(\Phi) = \sum_{ij} < \boldsymbol{\varphi}_i, \boldsymbol{\psi}_j > = \sum_{ij} |\boldsymbol{\varphi}_i^T \boldsymbol{\psi}_j|. \tag{9.6}$$

Since the basis matrix Ψ is usually a predefined constant matrix, e.g., a discrete wavelet transform (DWT) matrix, the *coherence measurement* defined in Eq. (9.6) is a weighted L1 norm of the matrix variable Φ. Given that Φ is determined by the kernel matrix $\mathbf{W}$ as in Eq. (9.4), the function $\mathcal{R}_{\mathbf{W}}$ is differentiable with respect to $\mathbf{W}$; therefore we can use Eq. (9.6) as regularization and estimate the sensing matrix Φ by minimizing $\mathcal{R}_{\mathbf{W}}$.

In practice the coherence regularization term $\mathcal{R}_{\mathbf{W}}$ is used for estimating the kernels of the compressive convolutional layer. The values of $\mathbf{W}$ and Φ are calculated via a gradient descent training process. By reducing the coherence between Φ and Ψ the iterative training process can calculate the near-isometric sensing matrix Φ for effective compressive sensing.

In our framework the coherence regularization only optimizes the first layer weights. Supposing $\mathbf{W}^{(k)}$ is the kth convolution kernel in the first layer, the total loss for training the whole detection network can be defined as follows:

$$\begin{aligned}\mathcal{L}_{\text{total}} &= \mathcal{L}_{\text{detection}} + \beta \cdot \sum_k \mathcal{R}_{\mathbf{W}^{(k)}}(\Phi) \\ &= \mathcal{L}_{\text{detection}} + \beta \cdot \sum_k \sum_{ij} |\boldsymbol{\varphi}_i^{(k)T} \boldsymbol{\psi}_j|, \end{aligned} \tag{9.7}$$

where $\mathcal{L}_{\text{detection}}$ is the loss function of detection terms, and β is a trade-off parameter. The coherence measurement term is added to improve the performance of compressive sensing of the first layer. For different networks, $\mathcal{L}_{\text{detection}}$ has different forms originated from the proposed literature, but our proposed coherence regularization term is the same. In our experiment, we test on the YOLOv2 [10] and SSD [9] frameworks.

To construct the sensing matrix Φ for compressive sensing, based on the trained network, we select the *single* best kernel of the compressive convolutional layer that achieves the highest Peak Signal-to-Noise Ratio (PSNR) reconstruction performance on the testing set.

It is worth noting that the output feature maps of the compressive convolutional layer have the same dimension as the input image data. The dimension reduction process and the sampling ratio are controlled by the uniform pooling layer. Furthermore, we quantize the features of the uniform pooling layer as [48] to achieve higher compression ratios. The image compression ratio (CR) can be calculated as follows:

$$CR = \text{Sampling Ratio} \times (\frac{\text{Quantization Bit-Depth}}{\text{Original Bit-Depth}}), \qquad (9.8)$$

where the sampling ratio is usually below 50%, and the quantization bit-depth ranges from one to five bits in our experiments. The original bit-depth is 16 bits, which is the standard bit-depth of the raw format of camera images.

9.3 Hardware implementation and optimization

As one of our contribution, we designed the SensCamera, which is a prototyping wireless smart camera system optimized to perform efficient video image compression and object detection in real time. By reconfiguring the deep neural network software, the SensCamera may be applied to different applications.

Smart Camera Hardware Platform. The smart camera prototype is implemented using the Intel Arria10 SX160 FPGA device, which is a programmable system on chip (SoC). The architecture of the wireless SensCamera system using Intel FPGA device is shown in Fig. 9.3. The CPUs in the SoC are working at 1.2 GHz, and the FPGA has 8.8 Mb on-chip random access memory. The NPU module is a commercially-available Rainman accelerator implemented using the FPGA device, which is connected to 1 GB 533-MHz on-board memory with 3.8-GB/s fullduplex memory bandwidth. A 1280-720 pixel image sensor and a wireless WIFI transmitter are built in the SensCamera prototype.

The SensCamera is built using the off-the-shelf hardware platform. Fig. 9.4 shows the smart hardware prototype and the output image of

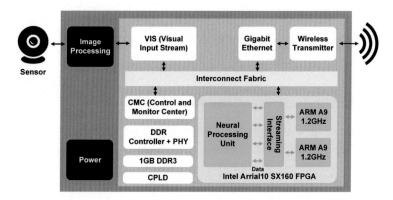

Figure 9.3 Architecture of the wireless SensCamera system implemented using Intel FPGA device. The off-the-shelf CNN inference hardware accelerator, i.e., the Neural Processing Unit, is deployed and reused for both object detection and image compression.

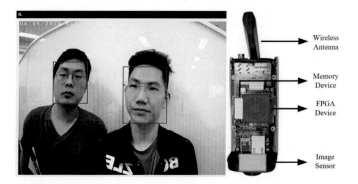

Figure 9.4 The prototyping SensCamera system is a wireless smart camera built for face detection and other object detection applications. The compressive convolutional network implemented using the FPGA device performs continuous object detection and image compression over the data stream captured by the image sensor.

the SensCamera. The smart camera hardware board is based on an Intel FPGA device with dual ARM CPUs and a commercially available neural processing unit (NPU) to accelerate the inference stage of a pretrained convolutional neural network. The computation logic of the proposed algorithm is implemented in the NPU with dedicated hardware. The design specification of the NPU is outside the scope of this paper; a more detailed information can be found in [50]. The dual ARM processors are used for parsing the deep neural network and controlling the data flow. The input image data are streamed into the NPU for object detection and image compression. Then the compressed images and the detection results (e.g., bounding box) are transmitted back to the CPU for packaging and wireless transmission.

9.4 Applications of SensCamera

A group of experiments were performed to evaluate the proposed method for both object detection and image compression. The hardware performance of the proposed algorithm running on the prototyping SensCamera system was also evaluated. Experiments showed that the proposed method shows better image compression performance than the conventional approaches while achieving competitively high accuracy and efficiency for object detection.

9.4.1 Experiment setting

To evaluate the effectiveness of the proposed method, our numerical experiments examined the proposed incoherent convolution approach with two popular CNN-based object detection frameworks, YOLO [10] and SSD [9]. The YOLO model has 23 layers, and the first layer has 32 convolution kernels. The SSD model has 22 layers, and the first layer has 64 convolution kernels. For each framework, the pretrained convolutional neural network parameters were used as the initial setting. We further trained the network on the VOC (2007+2012) training set (16551 images) and COCO training set (118287 images) by adding our proposed coherence regularization for 200000 iterations. We adopt the stochastic gradient descent (SGD) optimizer for optimization with a starting learning rate of 0.0001 and the momentum 0.9. The trade-off parameter β for coherence regularization was set to 0.0005. The features of the uniform pooling layer were quantized to one to five bits to compare different compression ratios.

We evaluated the proposed object detection and image compression method over four data sets: VOC (2007+2012), COCO, BSD100, and Set11 [51]. Both VOC and COCO are data sets widely used for evaluating object detection methods. The VOC data set contains 21530 images, including 27450 annotated objects and 6929 segmentations. The COCO data set contains 200000 images with a total of 80 categories. The BSD100 is a small data set containing 100 images, which is often used to evaluate the computationally expensive data-driven compressive sensing methods. The Set11 is a standard data set containing eleven images, which is widely used to evaluate the performance of image compression and reconstruction. As to test, for image compression, we conducted experiments on the testing sets VOC (2007+2012) (4952 images), BSD100 (100 images), and Set11 (11 images) data sets, only with those models trained on VOC (2007+2012) training set. For objection detection, we respectively conducted experiments on VOC (2007+2012) testing set (4952 images) and COCO testing set (40670 images).

To compare the CCN with other image compression methods, different measurements were adopted in our experiment, including the peak signal-to-noise ratio (PSNR) and the structural similarity index (SSIM). Given a bit depth of 8 bits, the values of PSNR in lossy images and video compression were generally distributed between 30 dB and 50 dB. For some IoT applications, a range of 20 dB to 25 dB can also be acceptable for wireless transmission. The SSIM was used to measure the similarity of two images in luminance, contrast and structure. Both PSNR and SSIM were widely used to evaluate the quality of image compression. For object detection, we calculated and compared the mean average precision (mAP), top-5 accuracy, and recall rate over the VOC and COCO test data sets.

The CCN is similar to the NuMax [12] and ADAGIO [14] methods, which are all data-driven near-isometric data embedding approaches. Generally, we can apply different back-end image reconstruction algorithms to recover the data compressed by these methods. Although it might not be the best solution, for fair comparison, we used the standard orthogonal match pursuit (OMP) algorithm for image reconstruction. As described in [49], the discrete wavelet transform (DWT) matrix was used as the basis matrix Ψ for the OMP algorithm to reconstruct images. In our experiment, the block size of the OMP algorithm was set to the default value of 16×16.

9.4.2 Performance of image compression

We compared the image compression performance of the CCN with other methods over the VOC, BSD100, and Set11 data sets. We compared the conventional method using Gaussian random matrices (GAUSS), the random convolution method (RandConv) [11], and the method based on sparse matrices (CS-SM) [46]. Besides, as a data-driven method, the CCN was also used to compare with the NuMax [12] and the recently proposed ADAGIO [14] algorithm. One kernel of the compressive convolutional layer was used for data embedding by the CCN. The standard OMP algorithm was used to reconstruct the images [49].

Table 9.1 The generalization experiment of the CCN-YOLO over VOC data sets and BSD100 data set at 0.33 sampling ratio.

Data Set	Train Set	Test Set	
	VOC Train	VOC Test	BSD100
PSNR	27.10 ± 3.90	26.54 ± 3.71	26.56 ± 2.98

Table 9.1 is a generalization experiment on the YOLO framework over VOC and BSD100 data sets at 0.33 sampling ratio. For VOC training set, we obtain 27.10 dB PSNR, VOC testing set with 26.54 dB, and BSD100 data set with 26.56 dB. It truly performs the best on the training set, associating it with the data-driven mechanism, whereas it achieves similar performance on the testing set and BSD100 data set. Though our approach calculates the compressive sensing matrix in a data-driven manner, the compressive sensing matrix is still with full-rank and near-isometric property, which is the basic principle of compressive sensing [39,40]. Thanks to the full-rank and near-isometric property, compressive sensing module can generalize well, regardless of the distribution shift among the training set and other data sets, just done as other data-driven compressive sensing methods [41–44].

Table 9.2 summarizes the experimental results of a fixed sampling ratio of 0.33 over the VOC and BSD100 data sets. For comparison, the original kernels of the YOLO were evaluated for data embedding. The experiment showed that the best kernel of the first convolutional layer of the YOLO model achieved 25.3 dB average PSNR for compressive sensing, which outperformed the random convolution approach (RandConv) by 2.1 dB [11]. By incorporating the coherence regularization the average PSNR of the CCN-YOLO convolution reached 26.5 dB. Overall, the CCN-YOLO was 2.7 dB ($\approx 26.54 - 23.89$ on VOC data set) to 5.2 dB ($\approx 26.56 - 21.32$ on BSD100 data set) higher than other compressive sensing approaches. Similar results were found for the CCN-SSD model, which achieved 25.2 dB average PSNR and 0.79 dB average SSIM over the VOC and BSD100 data sets, which were higher than the compared approaches.

Fig. 9.5 compares the results of four typical VOC images captured for people detection. The measurements of PSNR/SSIM are shown below each subpicture. Generally, the CCN-YOLO showed higher PSNR/SSIM compared with other approaches. The images compressed by the CCN also look better and are less noisy. Further examination of image details showed that the CCN images generally have higher sharpness in regions containing complex contexture.

Table 9.2 Image recovery quality over the BSD100 and VOC data sets at the fixed sampling ratio of 0.33.

Data Set	BSD100		VOC	
Method	PSNR	SSIM	PSNR	SSIM
CCN-YOLO	*26.56 ± 2.98*	*0.8192 ± 0.0550*	*26.54 ± 3.71*	*0.8786 ± 0.0745*
CCN-SSD	*25.19 ± 3.05*	*0.7872 ± 0.0620*	*25.46 ± 3.52*	*0.8253 ± 0.0524*
ADAGIO	22.42 ±1.75	0.6055 ± 0.0632	23.89 ± 3.38	0.6325 ± 0.0618
RandConv	22.31 ± 1.91	0.6243 ± 0.0642	22.21 ± 2.93	0.6608 ± 0.0671
CS-SM	21.39 ± 2.86	0.5954 ± 0.0941	21.46 ± 3.74	0.6217 ± 0.0521
GAUSS	21.32 ± 2.93	0.5921 ± 0.0976	22.48 ± 4.18	0.6409 ± 0.1188

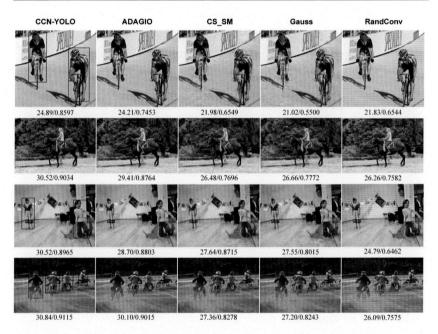

Figure 9.5 Comparing the proposed CCN approach with different compressive sensing approaches using Gaussian random matrices (GAUSS), random convolution (RandConv), CS-SM, and ADAGIO subsampling strategies at 0.33 sampling ratio. The image quality measurements of PSNR/SSIM are shown below each subpicture.

Compared to other data-driven compressive sensing approaches, the proposed CCN also shows much higher time efficiency for the training process. We performed numerical experiments on a computer equipped with Intel i7-6800k CPU and 32 GB memory. The images of BSD100 had 38400 pixels, which made it difficult to run the NuMax algorithm on a conventional computer. For the NuMax algorithm, we split the images into 16 × 16 blocks. Table 9.3 lists the training times of the CCN-YOLO,

Table 9.3 Training time (second) of the examined data-driven compressive sensing approaches over the BSD100 image set.

Number of images	10	20	40	100
NuMax	267	838	1537	4460
ADAGIO	0.743	2.041	7.263	45.782
CCN-YOLO	3.034	6.072	12.325	31.069
CCN-SSD	2.710	5.419	10.835	27.016

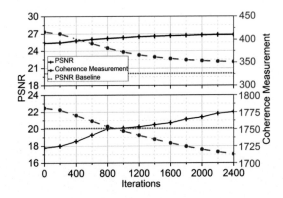

Figure 9.6 The change of coherence measurement and average PSNR during the training process over the VOC data set. Only the top two kernels with the highest PSNR are shown here to save space.

CCN-SSD, ADAGIO, and NuMax. NuMax consumed more than 4000 seconds to train, even though the data set only contained 100 images. The ADAGIO algorithm optimized the NuMax algorithm by relaxing the SDP problem into an eigenvalue problem. However, when more than 100 images were used for training, its efficiency was still lower than the proposed CCN. Due to the unaffordable complexity of memory and time, the ADAGIO algorithm was impractical for large-scale COCO data set.

The coherence measurement of the proposed method was also examined in our experiments. Fig. 9.6 shows the change of coherence measurement and average PSNR during the training process of the CCN over the VOC data set. With the regularization weight set as 0.0005, the coherence measurement continuously decreased in the first two thousand iterations, and the PSNR of the compressed images had an improvement of 1.2 dB to over 4.0 dB. Fig. 9.6 shows the results obtained with the top two kernels in the compressive convolutional layer. This experiment may prove the effectiveness of coherence regularization for image compression.

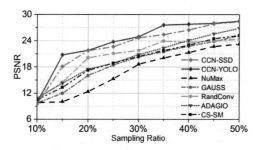

Figure 9.7 Image reconstruction PSNR for the examined approaches over the BSD100 data set.

Fig. 9.7 compares different compressive sensing methods with the sampling ratio ranging from 0.1 to 0.5. The NuMax and ADAGIO algorithms need to solve a semidefinite program and eigenvalue problems, which were difficult to be applied to large-scale data sets, so this experiment was only performed over the small BSD100 data set. In general, the CCN achieved the highest average PSNR over the BSD100 data set.

We also compared the CCN approach with the standard JPEG and JPEG2000 approaches for image compression. Different compression ratios were realized by setting a different quantization bit-depth. In our experiment the sampling ratio was fixed at 0.33, and we adopted a different quantization bit-depth of one to five bits respectively for 0.02–0.10 compression ratios. Table 9.4 lists the PSNR and SSIM of image reconstruction under different compression ratios. Compared with the JPEG approach, the CCN had 0.37 dB ($\approx 33.31 - 32.94$) to 3.49 dB ($\approx 26.13 - 22.64$) higher reconstruction PSNR, and the CCN also had comparable performance with the JPEG2000 at low compression ratios.

9.4.3 Performance of object detection

Two widely applied CNN-based object detection frameworks, the YOLO [10] and SSD [9], were examined to evaluate the proposed method for object detection. Table 9.5 summarizes the results of inference accuracy and speed, which are compared with different variants of R-CNN, SSD, and YOLO models. For a better comparison of the inference speed, the number of frames processed by the proposed method per second was evaluated over a computer with Intel i7-6800k CPU and 32 GB memory.

The experiment showed that, generally, the incorporation of image compression does not affect the performance of object detection. Specif-

Table 9.4 Comparing image reconstruction PSNR/SSIM of the CCN approach with the standard JPEG and JPEG2000 approaches over the Set11 data set (sampling ratio is fixed at 0.33 and quantization bit-depth ranges from one to five bits).

Compression Ratio	Method	Monarch	Barbara	Boats	Cameraman	House	Lena	Average
0.02	CCN-YOLO	24.55/0.7275	24.99/0.7245	26.55/0.7566	25.64/0.8200	28.91/0.8366	26.16/0.7459	26.13/0.7685
	JPEG	21.12/0.6259	21.92/0.5364	22.84/0.6189	22.27/0.6036	25.01/0.7293	22.69/0.6096	22.64/0.6206
	JPEG2000	24.01/0.7605	25.40/0.7042	26.86/0.7549	25.64/0.7495	31.15/0.8302	27.50/0.8058	26.76/0.7675
0.04	CCN-YOLO	28.06/0.8282	28.25/0.8452	30.33/0.8483	28.95/0.8884	32.89/0.9090	30.11/0.8518	29.76/0.8618
	JPEG	23.80/0.7340	25.02/0.7086	27.29/0.7804	26.19/0.7876	32.08/0.8497	28.21/0.8188	27.10/0.7799
	JPEG2000	27.47/0.8668	28.83/0.8528	30.33/0.8557	28.87/0.8251	34.63/0.8744	30.83/0.8797	30.16/0.8591
0.06	CCN-YOLO	30.66/0.8861	29.82/0.8992	32.53/0.8964	30.75/0.9220	35.88/0.9454	32.53/0.9051	32.03/0.9050
	JPEG	27.02/0.8430	27.38/0.8347	29.97/0.8554	28.29/0.8485	34.43/0.8899	31.02/0.8927	29.69/0.8607
	JPEG2000	29.93/0.9016	31.51/0.9057	32.92/0.9055	30.93/0.8770	36.45/0.9023	33.29/0.9184	32.51/0.9018
0.08	CCN-YOLO	32.04/0.9154	30.31/0.9169	33.58/0.9166	31.43/0.9351	37.17/0.9592	33.63/0.9254	33.03/0.9276
	JPEG	28.82/0.8875	29.62/0.8908	31.93/0.8963	29.82/0.8800	35.61/0.9098	32.75/0.9225	31.42/0.8978
	JPEG2000	31.81/0.9321	33.40/0.9351	34.90/0.9328	32.75/0.9049	37.82/0.9310	35.29/0.9382	34.33/0.9290
0.10	CCN-YOLO	32.43/0.9253	30.46/0.9215	33.77/0.9218	31.64/0.9394	37.65/0.9632	33.89/0.9302	33.31/0.9336
	JPEG	30.29/0.9156	31.54/0.9232	33.42/0.9195	31.18/0.9028	36.87/0.9297	34.33/0.9415	32.94/0.9221
	JPEG2000	33.31/0.9441	34.73/0.9477	36.23/0.9471	34.46/0.9268	39.27/0.9482	36.66/0.9506	35.78/0.9441

Table 9.5 Comparing the proposed CCN with other CNN-based methods for object detection. Both accuracy measurement of mean average precision (mAP (%)) on VOC and COCO (IOU=0.5) and efficiency measurement of frames per second (FPS) are listed.

Training Set	Method	mAP	FPS
VOC 2007+2012	Fast R-CNN	70.0	0.5
	Faster R-CNN ResNet	76.4	5
	SSD	74.3	46
	YOLOv1	63.4	45
	YOLOv2	78.6	40
	CCN-YOLO	**78.1**	**40**
	CCN-SSD	**74.0**	**46**
COCO trainval	Fast R-CNN	35.9	0.5
	Faster R-CNN ResNet	45.3	5
	SSD	41.2	46
	YOLOv2	44.0	40
	CCN-YOLO	**43.8**	**40**
	CCN-SSD	**41.1**	**46**

ically, the CCN-YOLO model achieved a mean average precision (mAP) of 78.1% over the VOC data set, almost the same as the original YOLOv2 model. Over the top five classes of the VOC data set, CCN-YOLO also achieved a competitively high 92.8% average accuracy and a comparable 86.6% recall rate. Considering that the average accuracy of the top five classes and the recall rate of the YOLOv2 model over the VOC data set were 93.3% and 86.8%, respectively, the CCN suffered almost no loss of performance compared to the original YOLO model. Similar results were found for the CCN-SSD model, which suffered almost no loss of accuracy and inference speed compared to the original SSD model over the VOC and COCO data sets.

9.4.4 Performance of the SensCamera system

The proposed CCN is a compressive-sensing-enabled convolutional neural network. The experiment showed that as a unified approach, the CCN was three times more efficient than the conventional implementations that used different components for compressive sensing and object detection. Table 9.6 compares the combined latency of image compression and object detection of the compared approaches. The proposed method is compared with the conventional strategies that a YOLO model or a SSD model is

Table 9.6 Comparing the inference time (second) of the proposed single-stage CCN approach with conventional dual-stage approaches.

Block Size	16×16	32×32	64×64	128×128
CCN-YOLO	2.82	2.82	2.82	2.82
Original YOLO	2.81	2.81	2.81	2.81
GAUSS+YOLO	8.81	9.25	11.65	14.15
ADAGIO+YOLO	8.81	9.24	11.67	14.13
CS-SM+YOLO	8.80	9.21	11.47	13.69
CCN-SSD	2.45	2.45	2.45	2.45
Original SSD	2.44	2.44	2.44	2.44
GAUSS+SSD	8.44	8.88	11.28	13.78
ADAGIO+SSD	8.44	8.87	11.30	13.76
CS-SM+SSD	8.43	8.84	11.10	13.32

performing *object detection side-by-side with a compressive sensing module* using different types of sensing matrices. It is worth noting that the conventional compressive sensing approaches require $O(\frac{M \times N}{B})$ floating-point multiplications at the front end for data embedding, and the complexity of these strategies depends on the block size B. On the other hand, the CCN models need much fewer multiplications, and it is 3.1–5.5 times more efficient than the conventional approaches.

The SensCamera was implemented as a prototyping wireless smart camera system with an integrated CCN-SSD algorithm for object detection and image compression. The camera was built with a 1280-720 pixel RGB image sensor, which captured video images at the speed of 25 frames per second (FPS). Frame by frame, the video image was streamed into the FPGA device, which was optimized for power-efficient implementation of the CCN-SSD algorithm. The experiment showed that the prototyping SensCamera could process 20–25 FPS, which was adequate for a wide range of IoT and surveillance applications. Further examination showed that the performance metric of FPS was partially affected by the number of potential objects detected in the image.

Fig. 9.8 shows the SensCamera running in real-time for object detection and image compression. Thanks to algorithm-level and hardware-level optimization, the peak power consumption of the SensCamera was as low as 13.97 watts. The FPGA implementation of the CCN-SSD algorithm consumed 7.2 watts on average.

Figure 9.8 The SensCamera manages to perform object detection and image compression over 1280 × 720 video images at nearly real-time with less than 14 W power consumption.

References

[1] S. Fleck, W. Strasser, Smart camera based monitoring system and its application to assisted living, Proceedings of the IEEE 96 (10) (2008) 1698–1714.

[2] J.F. Romanowich, Methods and apparatus related to improved surveillance using a smart camera, US Patent 8,531,521 (September 2013).

[3] Y. Sun, Y. Chen, X. Wang, X. Tang, Deep learning face representation by joint identification–verification, in: Proceedings of International Conference on Neural Information Processing Systems, 2014, pp. 1988–1996.

[4] G. Amato, F. Carrara, F. Falchi, C. Gennaro, C. Vairo, Car parking occupancy detection using smart camera networks and deep learning, in: Proceedings of IEEE Symposium on Computers and Communication, 2016, pp. 1212–1217.

[5] A. Loquercio, A.I. Maqueda, C.R. Del-Blanco, D. Scaramuzza, DroNet: Learning to fly by driving, IEEE Robotics and Automation Letters 3 (2) (2018) 1088–1095.

[6] R. Girshick, J. Donahue, T. Darrell, J. Malik, Rich feature hierarchies for accurate object detection and semantic segmentation, in: Proceedings of IEEE Conference on Computer Vision and Pattern Recognition, 2014, pp. 580–587.

[7] R. Girshick, Fast R-CNN, in: Proceedings of IEEE International Conference on Computer Vision, 2015, pp. 1440–1448.

[8] S. Ren, K. He, R. Girshick, J. Sun, Faster R-CNN: Towards real-time object detection with region proposal networks, IEEE Transactions on Pattern Analysis and Machine Intelligence 39 (6) (2015) 1137–1149.

[9] W. Liu, D. Anguelov, D. Erhan, C. Szegedy, S. Reed, C.-Y. Fu, A.C. Berg, SSD: Single shot multibox detector, in: Proceedings of European Conference on Computer Vision, 2016, pp. 21–37.

[10] J. Redmon, A. Farhadi, YOLO9000: better, faster, stronger, in: Proceedings of IEEE Conference on Computer Vision and Pattern Recognition, 2017, pp. 7263–7271.

[11] J. Romberg, Compressive sensing by random convolution, SIAM Journal on Imaging Sciences 2 (4) (2009) 1098–1128.

[12] C. Hegde, A.C. Sankaranarayanan, W. Yin, R.G. Baraniuk, NuMax: A convex approach for learning near–isometric linear embeddings, IEEE Transactions on Signal Processing 63 (22) (2015) 6109–6121.

[13] L. Baldassarre, Y.H. Li, J. Scarlett, B. Gözcü, I. Bogunovic, V. Cevher, Learning-based compressive subsampling, IEEE Journal of Selected Topics in Signal Processing 10 (4) (2016) 809–822.

[14] J. Blasiok, C.E. Tsourakakis, Adagio: Fast data-aware near-isometric linear embeddings, in: Proceedings of IEEE International Conference on Data Mining, 2016, pp. 31–40.

[15] A. Mousavi, R.G. Baraniuk, Learning to invert: Signal recovery via deep convolutional networks, in: Proceedings of IEEE International Conference on Acoustics, Speech and Signal Processing, 2017, pp. 2272–2276.

[16] A. Mousavi, G. Dasarathy, R.G. Baraniuk, DeepCodec: Adaptive sensing and recovery via deep convolutional neural networks, arXiv:1707.03386 [abs].

[17] X. Lu, W. Dong, P. Wang, G. Shi, X. Xie, ConvCSNet: A convolutional compressive sensing framework based on deep learning, arXiv:1801.10342 [abs].

[18] M. Iliadis, L. Spinoulas, A.K. Katsaggelos, Deep fully-connected networks for video compressive sensing, Digital Signal Processing 72 (2018) 9–18.

[19] K. Xu, Z. Zhang, F. Ren, LAPRAN: A scalable Laplacian pyramid reconstructive adversarial network for flexible compressive sensing reconstruction, in: Proceedings of the European Conference on Computer Vision, 2018, pp. 485–500.

[20] Y. Wu, M. Rosca, T. Lillicrap, Deep compressed sensing, in: Proceedings of the International Conference on Machine Learning, 2019, pp. 6850–6860.

[21] Z. Chen, X. Hou, L. Shao, C. Gong, X. Qian, Y. Huang, S. Wang, Compressive sensing multi-layer residual coefficients for image coding, IEEE Transactions on Circuits and Systems for Video Technology 30 (4) (2019) 1109–1120.

[22] S. Zhou, Y. He, Y. Liu, C. Li, J. Zhang, Multi-channel deep networks for block-based image compressive sensing, IEEE Transactions on Multimedia 23 (2021) 2627–2640.

[23] S. Tanwar, P. Patel, K. Patel, S. Tyagi, N. Kumar, M.S. Obaidat, An advanced internet of thing based security alert system for smart home, in: Proceedings of International Conference on Computer, Information and Telecommunication Systems, 2017, pp. 25–29.

[24] S. Latif, H. Afzaal, N.A. Zafar, Intelligent traffic monitoring and guidance system for smart city, in: Proceedings of International Conference on Computing, Mathematics and Engineering Technologies, 2018, pp. 1–6.

[25] S.-H. Lee, C.-S. Yang, A real time object recognition and counting system for smart industrial camera sensor, IEEE Sensors Journal 17 (8) (2017) 2516–2523.

[26] G. Amato, P. Bolettieri, D. Moroni, F. Carrara, L. Ciampi, G. Pieri, C. Gennaro, G.R. Leone, C. Vairo, A wireless smart camera network for parking monitoring, in: Proceedings of IEEE Globecom Workshops, 2018, pp. 1–6.

[27] V. Gokhale, J. Jin, A. Dundar, B. Martini, E. Culurciello, A 240 G-ops/s mobile co-processor for deep neural networks, in: Proceedings of IEEE Conference on Computer Vision and Pattern Recognition, 2014, pp. 682–687.

[28] C. Zhang, P. Li, G. Sun, Y. Guan, B. Xiao, J. Cong, Optimizing FPGA-based accelerator design for deep convolutional neural networks, in: Proceedings of ACM/SIGDA International Symposium on Field-Programmable Gate Arrays, 2015, pp. 161–170.

[29] N. Li, S. Takaki, Y. Tomiokay, H. Kitazawa, A multistage dataflow implementation of a deep convolutional neural network based on FPGA for high-speed object recognition, in: Proceedings of IEEE Southwest Symposium on Image Analysis and Interpretation, 2016, pp. 165–168.

[30] J. Qiu, J. Wang, S. Yao, K. Guo, B. Li, E. Zhou, J. Yu, T. Tang, N. Xu, S. Song, et al., Going deeper with embedded FPGA platform for convolutional neural network, in: Proceedings of ACM/SIGDA International Symposium on Field-Programmable Gate Arrays, 2016, pp. 26–35.

[31] X. Zhou, S. Li, F. Tang, S. Hu, Z. Lin, L. Zhang, DaNoC: An efficient algorithm and hardware codesign of deep neural networks on chip, IEEE Transactions on Neural Networks and Learning Systems 29 (7) (2017) 3176–3187.

[32] R. Zhao, X. Niu, Y. Wu, W. Luk, Q. Liu, Optimizing CNN-based object detection algorithms on embedded FPGA platforms, in: Proceedings of International Symposium on Applied Reconfigurable Computing, 2017, pp. 255–267.

[33] H. Mao, S. Yao, T. Tang, B. Li, J. Yao, Y. Wang, Towards real-time object detection on embedded systems, IEEE Transactions on Emerging Topics in Computing 6 (3) (2016) 417–431.

[34] T. Wiegand, G.J. Sullivan, G. Bjontegaard, A. Luthra, Overview of the H.264/AVC video coding standard, IEEE Transactions on Circuits and Systems for Video Technology 13 (7) (2003) 560–576.

[35] G.J. Sullivan, J.-R. Ohm, W.-J. Han, T. Wiegand, Overview of the high efficiency video coding (HEVC) standard, IEEE Transactions on Circuits and Systems for Video Technology 22 (12) (2012) 1649–1668.

[36] Y. Chen, D. Murherjee, J. Han, A. Grange, Y. Xu, Z. Liu, S. Parker, C. Chen, H. Su, U. Joshi, et al., An overview of core coding tools in the AV1 video codec, in: Proceedings of Picture Coding Symposium, 2018, pp. 41–45.

[37] D. Mukherjee, J. Bankoski, A. Grange, J. Han, J. Koleszar, P. Wilkins, Y. Xu, R. Bultje, The latest open-source video codec VP9 – an overview and preliminary results, in: Proceedings of Picture Coding Symposium, 2013, pp. 390–393.

[38] E.J. Candès, J. Romberg, T. Tao, Robust uncertainty principles: Exact signal reconstruction from highly incomplete frequency information, IEEE Transactions on Information Theory 52 (2) (2006) 489–509.

[39] D.L. Donoho, Compressed sensing, IEEE Transactions on Information Theory 52 (4) (2006) 1289–1306.

[40] E.J. Candès, M.B. Wakin, An introduction to compressive sampling, IEEE Signal Processing Magazine 25 (2) (2008) 21–30.

[41] E.J. Candes, T. Tao, Near-optimal signal recovery from random projections: Universal encoding strategies?, IEEE Transactions on Information Theory 52 (12) (2006) 5406–5425.

[42] X. Song, X. Peng, J. Xu, G. Shi, F. Wu, Distributed compressive sensing for cloud-based wireless image transmission, IEEE Transactions on Multimedia 19 (6) (2017) 1351–1364.

[43] Z. Chen, X. Hou, X. Qian, C. Gong, Efficient and robust image coding and transmission based on scrambled block compressive sensing, IEEE Transactions on Multimedia 20 (7) (2017) 1610–1621.

[44] X. Yuan, R. Haimi-Cohen, Image compression based on compressive sensing: End-to-end comparison with JPEG, IEEE Transactions on Multimedia 22 (11) (2020) 2889–2904.

[45] X. Zhou, L. Xu, S. Liu, Y. Lin, L. Zhang, C. Zhuo, An efficient compressive convolutional network for unified object detection and image compression, in: Proceedings of the AAAI Conference on Artificial Intelligence, vol. 33, 2019, pp. 5949–5956.

[46] A. Gilbert, P. Indyk, Sparse recovery using sparse matrices, Proceedings of the IEEE 98 (6) (2010) 937–947.

[47] R. Baraniuk, Compressive sensing [lecture notes], IEEE Signal Processing Magazine 24 (2007) 118–121.

[48] R. Gong, X. Liu, S. Jiang, T. Li, P. Hu, J. Lin, F. Yu, J. Yan, Differentiable soft quantization: Bridging full-precision and low-bit neural networks, in: Proceedings of the International Conference on Computer Vision, 2019, pp. 4852–4861.

[49] J.A. Tropp, A.C. Gilbert, Signal recovery from random measurements via orthogonal matching pursuit, IEEE Transactions on Information Theory 53 (12) (2007) 4655–4666.

[50] CoreRain, Rainman accelerator, retrieved from http://www.corerain.com/product.
[51] K. Kulkarni, S. Lohit, P. Turaga, R. Kerviche, A. Ashok, ReconNet: Non-iterative reconstruction of images from compressively sensed measurements, in: Proceedings of the IEEE Conference on Computer Vision and Pattern Recognition, 2016, pp. 449–458.

Index

Printed in the United States
by Baker & Taylor Publisher Services